SOCCER SPEED

3S™ System

BY VERN GAMBETTA

gambetta
SPORTS TRAINING SYSTEMS

Printed in the United States of America

ISBN: 1-879627-03-5

gambetta
SPORTS TRAINING SYSTEMS

800-671-4045
www.gambetta.com

Acknowledgements

Steve Myrland who so graciously took the time early in the process to help organize and edit the book. He also wrote the descriptions of the speed/agility ladder drills.

Thomas Rongen for giving me the opportunity to work in professional soccer with both the Mutiny and the Revolution.

Steve Sampson for providing me with the opportunity to work with the World Cup team.

Roy Wegerle whose professionalism, hard work and dedication in preparation for the World Cup was an inspiration.

Anson Dorrance and the UNC women who showed me just how important speed is in soccer.

All the youth players and clubs that I have worked with—who proved that the concepts outlined in the book work at all levels of competition.

Lance Duggan, Richard Hynes and Reiss Holsbeke who patiently posed for the pictures and who survived the 1998 "Burn With Vern Breakfast Club."

Above all, Kristen Gambetta, my favorite soccer player, who has applied all the concepts to help make herself a better player.

TABLE OF CONTENTS

Mission

Speed is a motor task which can be learned and improved through practice like any other motor skill. In soccer, this is accomplished by learning correct movement mechanics without the ball. During training, it is necessary to recreate every speed and quickness situation or position that can occur in a game and rehearse those movements. Perfect the movements without the ball; then add the ball to apply the speed. Speed training demands the highest intensity and concentration! The game should have no surprises in terms of speed and power.

Soccer Speed Program Goals:

1 Integrate all aspects of speed into your existing training program! Make the best better.

2 Teach correct execution & routine of exercises.

3 Improve all aspects of speed as it relates to the game of soccer.
    a) Straight Ahead
    b) Lateral Speed & Agility
    c) Speed of Decision Making

Speed Wins!

Speed Demands of Soccer

Fundamentally, soccer is a high speed skill game of quick starts & quick stops played in a climate of fatigue. The main endurance demands are for speed endurance. In order to endure speed it is necessary to have speed.

- **Straight Ahead Speed** - The average straight ahead sprint in soccer is twelve yards. Most sprints are significantly shorter.
- **Change of Direction** - Thousands of different movements occur during the course of the game.
- **Obstacle Avoidance** - To be an effective player it is necessary to stay on your feet avoiding tackles or players who have fallen in front of you with a minimum loss of speed.
- **Spatial Awareness** - This is awareness of your position and space in relation to everyone else on the field.
- **Speed of Decision Making** - All the speed in world will have no effect if you are unable to rapidly assess the situation and make a decision without compromising the speed of play.

In summary, soccer is a game of speed/power & skill played in a climate of fatigue. Without speed and power, the most skilled and fit player, ultimately, will not be able to achieve at the highest levels.

"Contrary to other athletes, soccer players need to have a high rhythm of movement. They constantly need to accelerate and decelerate quickly, run curves, weave and turn. These are the skills that have to be trained."

Louis van Gaal
Former Ajax Coach

THE BASIS OF SOCCER SPEED DEVELOPMENT – LEARNING TO MOVE

Soccer success is built on sound fundamentals. The most fundamental is movement skill. Typically, movement skills are learned through free play and reinforced with more formal instruction. In our society, free play has almost disappeared. To address this change in lifestyle, coaches must incorporate fundamental movement skills as a routine portion of the workout. These fundamental movement skills are the basis for more complex soccer specific movements. Soccer movements are a series of linked fundamental movement skills. If an athlete has a rich repertoire of motor skills to draw from, it is easier to acquire soccer skill, and the athlete will be less prone to injury because the body is prepared for all movements.

The fundamental movement skills consist of:

Locomotor Skills: are skills that move the body from one place to another. They consist of walking, running, leaping, hopping, & jumping.

Nonlocomotor Skills: are movements that involve little or no movement of the base of support. Nonlocomotor skills are also sometimes called stability skills. They consist of movements like swaying, turning, twisting, swinging, and balancing.

Manipulative Skills: are movements that focus on control of objects primarily using the hands and feet. They are both propulsive and receptive. Propulsive skills include striking, throwing and kicking. Receptive skills include catching and trapping.

Movement Awareness: includes the combination of abilities required to form an effective response to sensory information that is needed to perform a specific motor task.

Body Awareness: the knowledge of one's own body parts and their movement capabilities. The components of body awareness are:

Spatial Awareness: the ability to orient to other people and objects in space as well as how much space the body occupies. It is the sense of where other people are on the field.

Rhythmic Awareness: the ability to

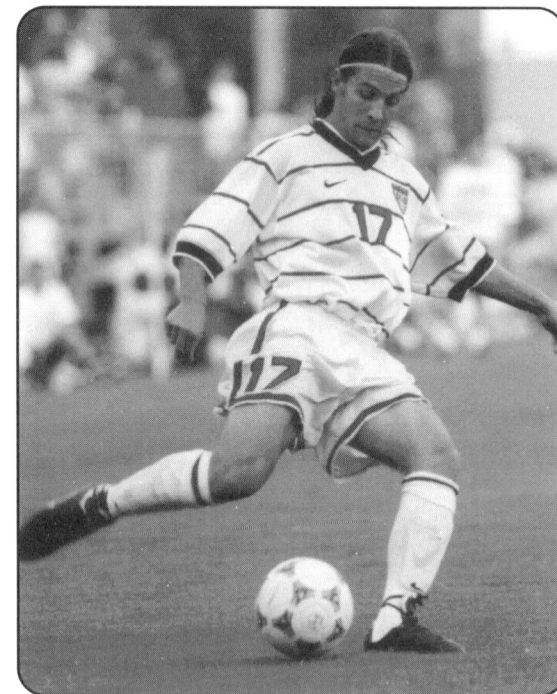

make movements that are repetitive and patterned resulting in balanced harmonious movement. Sometimes rhythmic movement is more important than speed.

Directional Awareness: the ability to discriminate the size of objects and their relation to each other. Directional awareness consists of laterality—awareness of right and left—and directionality—awareness of forward back, up and down, and various combinations.

Vestibular Awareness: provides information about the bodies relationship to gravity. Essentially, it is the basis for balance and body position.

Visual Awareness: the ability to receive and process visual stimuli. This is especially important for the goalkeeper, but necessary for all players.

Temporal Awareness: is the timing mechanism in the body. It is the ability to judge time.

Auditory Awareness: the ability to discriminate, associate and interpret sound. This is important in judging distance and communicating with teammates.

Tactile Awareness: the ability to discriminate through touch and feel. This is very important in reading and judging pressure from a defender and being able to move with or away from that pressure.

The way to develop movement abilities is through play and self discovery as a child grows and develops. In a formal sense, the best way to include these movement skills is in a structured warm-up that places demands on the various fundamental movements as a lead-up to the soccer-specific movements to follow. It is also advisable to structure specific speed workouts both with, and without the ball that incorporate as many of these fundamental skills as possible. The optimum order of development is to first learn the movement without regard to speed. Then, increase the speed of the movement while paying particular attention to maintaining the precision of the movement. The third step is to change the movements or do them under slightly different conditions. The fourth step is to follow with fundamental soccer skills based on the movement skill.

Fundamental movement skills developed at younger ages become automated and part of a reservoir of motor skills which can be called upon when learning specific soccer skills. *Speed must be incorporated first.* It is a motor quality that demands a high degree of coordination. It can be developed in a play environment using tag games and relays. Everything should be short and quick so that fatigue is not a factor. Look at the soccer skill and analyze it in the context of the prerequisite movement skills leading up to that skill. Then design a progression so that there is a smooth transition from one into the other. To insure long-term success, it is *necessary to acquire fundamental movement skills before specific soccer skills. Fundamental movement skill will significantly enhance the ability to learn to move faster.*

SOCCER SPEED COMPONENTS

STRAIGHT AHEAD SPEED (SAS)

Starting - Overcoming inertia from both standing and moving positions. The emphasis is on starting from different positions incorporating movement in order to imitate the demands of the game. Stationary starts are rare in soccer, except for the goalkeeper.

Acceleration - Acceleration is the rate of change of velocity that allows the player to reach maximum velocity in a minimum amount of time. It is getting to top speed. The ability to accelerate is essential to success in soccer.

Top Speed - Also called maximum speed. It is the highest speed that a player is capable of. This does not come into play very often in the course of a game, but it is still important.

Deceleration - The act of slowing down. The ability to slow down under control is critical for success in soccer.

Speed In Cooperation - Matching the individual player's speed with other players to create optimum team speed.

LATERAL SPEED AND AGILITY (LSA)

Recognition/Reaction - Recognizing the correct stimulus (situation) and reacting in the shortest time possible. The primary stimulus in soccer is visual; therefore, most of the practice should be reacting to visual cues. Good reaction/recognition ability is essential for success.

Decision Making Speed - Moving to space, deciding where to pass or move in the shortest time possible while reading and assessing game situations. This, coupled with reaction and recognition, are very important for game awareness and game speed.

Balance/ Body Awareness - Maintaining control of one's own center of gravity while knowing where the body and its parts are at all times. This is a dynamic, not a static quality. It is key to applying speed to soccer skill and prevention of injury.

Footwork - Quickness and control of the feet and their movement to carry over to movement with and without the ball. The game is played with the feet: without good footwork it is impossible to be a good player.

Change of Direction - The ability to change direction of the body's center of gravity as quickly as possible with control. Soccer is a game of constant directional changes with and without the ball.

Obstacle Avoidance - The ability to avoid other players feet, tackles, and bodies

lying on the ground.

ACCELERATION

Acceleration is the key to soccer performance. It is the most trainable component of speed. Acceleration is the rate of change of velocity that allows the player to reach maximum speed in a minimum amount of time. It takes a sprinter between 30m and 60m in a 100 meter race to reach top speed. Seldom does a soccer player have that much time or space based on the speed demands of the game.

Acceleration mechanics should be evaluated and trained in the context of Posture, Arm Action, and Leg Action (PAL):

Posture is the position and alignment of the body—especially the head and trunk. Body lean comes from the ankle, not the waist. This position is dynamic and changes with each step from the starting position on up to and through top speed. It also changes with and without contact with the ball.

Arm Action is the position and amplitude of movement of the arms and hands. The arms help to produce force and aid in balance so that force is properly applied against the ground. During acceleration, the emphasis is on driving the arms down and back to apply force against the ground.

Leg Action focuses on the action of the foot, ankle, knee and hip. The leg action in acceleration is a driving action characterized by the feeling of pushing back behind the body during the initial steps. The emphasis is on backside mechanics - what occurs behind the body. The pushing action occurs from the start through the first four to six steps. To cue the correct pattern, it is helpful to use the following verbal cues:

1st Step>2nd Step>3rd Step>4th Step>5th & 6th Step
Push>>> Push>>> Push>>> Push>>> Hips> Tall.

To ensure correct force application and proper transition to top speed, it is necessary to have a correct pattern of acceleration. The pattern consists of each succeeding step increasing in length until full stride length is achieved. Most young players try to take steps that are too long, thinking that they will get to top speed sooner. The opposite occurs: they end up stumbling and reaching which slows them down and puts them at greater risk of injury. Steve Myrland, Conditioning Coach at the University of Wisconsin, uses the analogy of someone driving a stick shift in a car trying to go from first gear to fifth gear. Inevitably the car will stall. The same thing happens to the athlete who tries to go too fast, too soon without shifting gears.

The goal is to create a positive shin angle, *(see photo)* the angle formed by the shin and ground with the foot contacting the ground behind the center of gravity on the first two steps, and then as close as possible under the center of gravity after that. A positive shin angle allows for proper force application and control of the stride. The opposite is a negative shin angle *(see photo)* where the foot contacts the ground in front of the center of gravity. This results in a braking action which causes the player to pull over the ground contact foot. This is highly inefficient and predisposes the player to injury. To create a positive shin angle on the first step and each succeeding step, it is imperative to get the foot back down on the ground as fast as possible.

Each aspect of acceleration mechanics (Posture, Arm Action, Leg Action) has a profound effect upon the other two areas. If one is off, there will be a compensation in the other two. It has been my experience that breakdowns generally occur in the enumerated order. Poor posture will lead to compensations in arm action and a reduced amplitude of movement of the legs.

After the start, the player accelerates by increasing both stride length and frequency. Ultimately, speed is determined by an optimum combination of these two components. This optimum combination is another factor which is profoundly affected by a correct pattern of acceleration. Of the two factors, stride frequency is the most important in soccer performance. The optimum combination of stride length and frequency is highly impacted by the pattern established in the first few steps. Enhanced strength will improve both frequency and stride length. Improved strength enables a player to produce higher amounts of force more quickly decreasing ground contact time.

The high intensity demand of speed development primarily taxes the nervous system which is "the central command" system of the body. This must receive careful consideration when designing a training program as it is the dominant influence on performance. Care must be taken to design exercises and training sessions that facilitate the recruitment of the appropriate motor units to produce the greatest rate of force production in the shortest possible time. In a sport like soccer, which is played in a climate of fatigue, consideration of nervous system demand gets lost in the search for better fitness. Due to improper training design and/or frequent games, many athletes are in a constant state of nervous system fatigue. A general training rule is to allow twice the recovery time for central nervous system work as for energy system work. This can be accomplished by care-

Positive Shin Angle

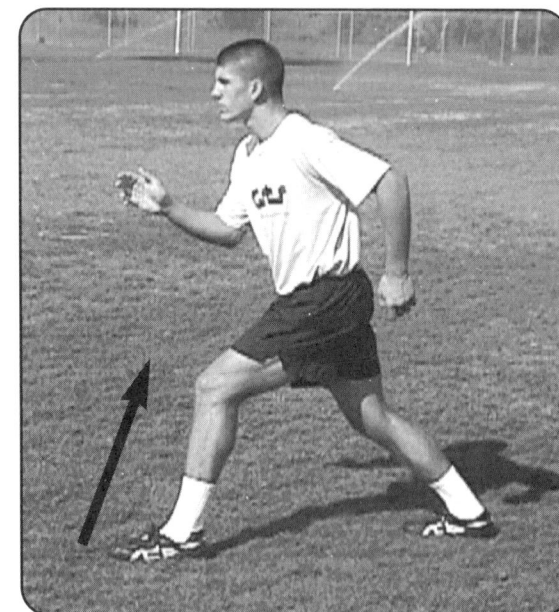

Negative Shin Angle

fully meshing the speed development and lateral speed and agility with skill, tactics and strategic development. Failure to observe this results in poor performance and frequent injuries to muscles and tendons.

Acceleration improvement is definitely linked to improvement in power: The capacity to produce the greatest amount of force in the shortest possible time. The strongest athletes spend less time on the ground and have longer strides which they are able to repeat with greater frequency. Maximal contractile strength is required at the start and the early stages of acceleration (up to 7.5 m/sec). At this point, the requirement begins to shift to elastic strength which is dependent on the stretch shortening cycle of muscular contraction. Contractile strength is most impacted by resistance work including weight training, harness running, and sled pulls. The elastic phase is impacted by plyometric work consisting of hurdle jumps, hopping, and bounding where ground contact is minimized.

Maturation plays a significant role in the perfection of acceleration skills. Many technical problems that occur in young players are due to the lack of physical maturity. This is mainly due to weak joint stabilization strength and core strength, and is manifested as poor posture. As the athlete matures, gains strength and improves body awareness, many technical faults are self corrected through growth and development.

Acceleration training should begin early (ages 8 - 12) during the so-called "skill hungry years" with games and playful drills. At this crucial age emphasize training methods that stimulate frequency of movement and increase speed with a focus on quality and intensity. Use a variety of starting positions to stimulate proprioceptive development. The training should be short, intense and playful.

The best way to learn how to accelerate is to accelerate. That may sound somewhat facetious but it is true. Therefore, it is important not to deviate too far from the whole action. Sprinting is a natural, rhythmic, flowing activity that cannot be made mechanical. A few drills done well and correctly applied are much better than a whole menu of drills done for drill sake. It is also important to remember that a drill which is good for a sprinter may not necessarily be good for a soccer player who has to quickly stop and receive a ball or change direction. Many of the high knee drills used in track are actually detrimental to soccer performance because they lengthen the stride and raise the players feet off the ground too much. Louis van Gaal, former coach of Ajax says "A soccer player who uses long strides will immediately fall prey to an opponent, because he will be easily deceived by a feint, or be knocked off balance." Soccer ability is enhanced by drills that teach athletes to get their feet on the ground.

ACTIVE WARM-UP

WARM-UP # 1
(Use before straight-ahead speed sessions.)

Jog 3 - 5 minutes
Easy run with an emphasis on good running mechanics. Be sure to run light and quietly.

Pendulum Leg Swings
See photos. 10 swings with each leg each movement. Hip flexion and extension. Hip abduction and adduction with internal and external rotation. Let the weight of the leg swing as a pendulum.

Do not kick the leg through. The pendulum swinging action will result in the leg raising progressively higher with each swing.

Active Stretch
a) *Hamstring — see photo*
Start lying on the back pull one knee to the chest. Extend the foreleg up and back while tensing the quad. Hold for one count and return to the starting position. Execute two repetitions at each of the following positions with each leg: 1) toe in 2) toe out 3) toe straight ahead.
b) *Psoas — see photo*
Start in a stride position with the back foot turned out at approximately forty-five degrees. Reach up and over with the arm on the side of the back foot, then extend the same arm up as high as possible. The next step is to take the same arm and reach across the body twisting

Active Stretch — Hamstring

Active Stretch — Psoas

Pendulum Leg Swings

Active Stretch — Crossover

Sidestep 2 x 30 yards

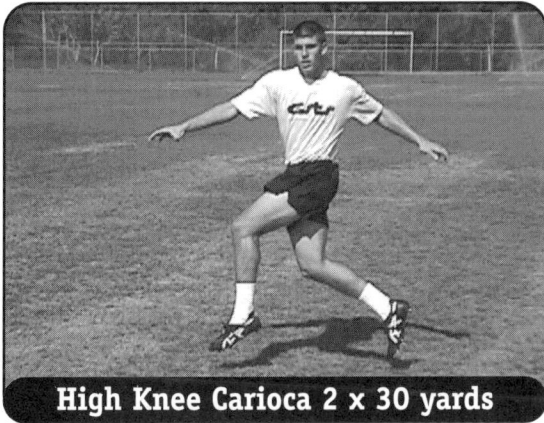
High Knee Carioca 2 x 30 yards

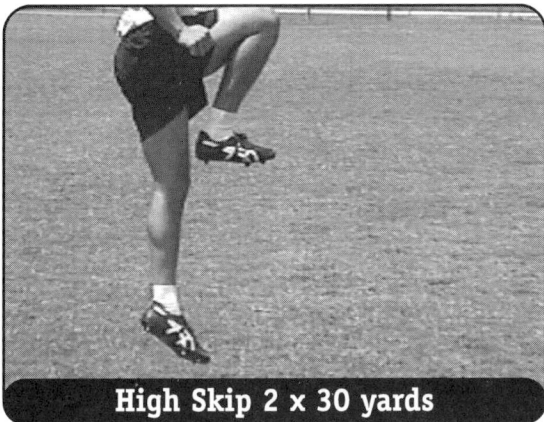
High Skip 2 x 30 yards

Carioca 2 x 30 yards Short Fast

Carioca 2 x 30 yards Low and Long

into the front leg. Hold each of the three positions for a three count.

c) *Crossover* — *see photo*

Start lying on the back with the arms extended out from the shoulders perpendicular from the body. Raise one leg up to perpendicular to the ground and bring the foot of that leg over to touch the hand of the opposite arm. Return the leg to the starting position repeating the movement in reverse. Repeat with the opposite leg.

Skip 2 x 30 yards
Low skip, concentrate on pushing off the big toe. Be sure to project forward, not up.

Crossover Skip 2 x 30 yards
Skip, crossing the right in front of the left and the left in front of the right.

Sidestep 2 x 30 yards — *see photo*
Step apart and extend arms out. Bring the legs and arms together.

Carioca 2 x 30 yards
Step behind and apart, step in front and apart. Emphasize being light on the feet.
a) *Short Fast* — *see photo*
Short quick steps with an emphasis on hips tall.
b) *Low and Long* — *see photo*
The opposite of the short and fast. Bend the knees. The movement should be deliberate with an emphasis on long strides.

High Knee Carioca 2 x 30 yards — *see photo*
Step behind and then drive the same leg up to the opposite armpit. Use the same leg one direction and the other leg in the opposite direction.

Backward Run 4 x 30 yards
Run backward emphasizing a full stride cycle. The heel should come to the butt and extend.

High Skip 2 x 30 yards —
see photo, previous page
Take off and extend the takeoff leg while driving the opposite knee and arm up. Land and take off the opposite leg. The emphasis in on driving up.

Warm-up #2

(Use before Lateral Speed & Agility sessions.)

Skipping with different arm action
a) Reach overhead using a windmill arm while skipping.
b) Reach overhead using both one arm & two arm.
c) Cross arms in front of the body.

Crossover Skip
Skip, crossing the right in front of the left and the left in front of the right.

Crazy Hips
Twist and skip as fast as possible with a wide range of motion at the hips.

Sidestep
Switch direction every two sidesteps.
a) *Angle Sidestep*
   Sidestep backward at a 45 degree angle after three sidesteps plant the outside foot and drop step to sidestep the opposite direction. Continue for thirty yards.
b) *Skipping Sidestep*
   Skipping off the back leg.

Carioca
Switch direction every two.
Angle Carioca — Carioca backward at a 45 degree angle plant the outside foot and drop step to carioca in the opposite direction. Repeat for thirty yards.

Plant & Cut 2 x 30 yds.
Three steps at a forty-five degree angle plant outside foot and drive off forty-five degrees opposite. Repeat planting and cutting off the other foot.

360s 2 x 30 yards
Turn 360 degrees right and 360 degrees left. Run our in a straight line. Repeat twice in thirty yards.

Backpedal into Sprint 2 x 30 yards
Backpedal for ten yards then turn and sprint.

Sprint into Backpedal 2 x 30 yards
Sprint twenty yards forward then turn and backpedal.

Warm-up #3

(Use before Shooting sessions)

Knee Hug
a) Pull up to chest with an emphasis on staying vertical — *see photo, opposite page*
b) Pull up to chest and ride out the back leg to project forward — *see photo, opposite page*

Swing Step — *see photo, opposite page*
Swing the leg out to the side

Half Volley — *see photo, opposite page*
Bent leg up and out under the armpit with a skip step.

High Step — *see photo, opposite page*
Bring knee up to chest height with each step.

High Step with Extension — *see photo, opposite page*
Bring knee up to chest height and extend the foreleg with each step.

Goose-step — *see photo, opposite page*
With each step bring the leg up straight up to hip height with each step
   a) *Circle Out* - Circle the foot out with each step.
   b) *Circle In* - Circle the foot in with each step.

Knee Hug (a)

Swing Step

High Step

Knee Hug (b)

Half Volley

High Step with extension

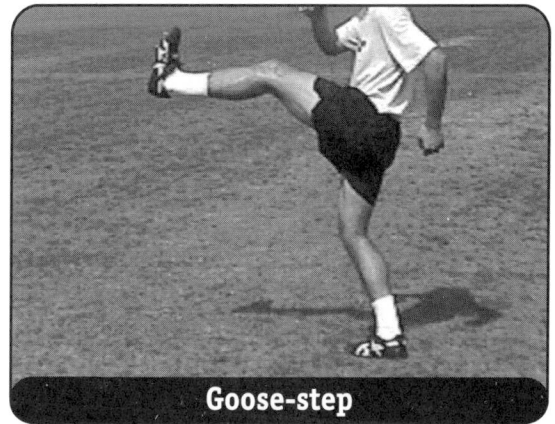

Goose-step

MINI BAND ROUTINE

Attach the band so it rests just above the ankle. Execute the desired motion while keeping constant tension on the band. *See photos.*

Sidestep x twenty each direction.

Walk forward/Back x twenty each direction.

Carioca x twenty each direction.

Monster Walk x twenty each direction.

Sidestep with band over instep x twenty each direction.

Walk -Forward/Back x twenty

Monster Walk x twenty

Sidestep x twenty

Carioca x twenty

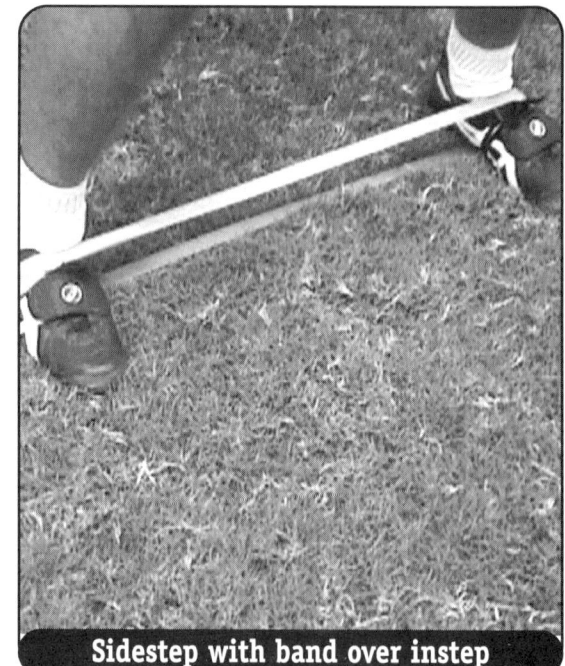

Sidestep with band over instep

HURDLE WALK ROUTINE

Over the top

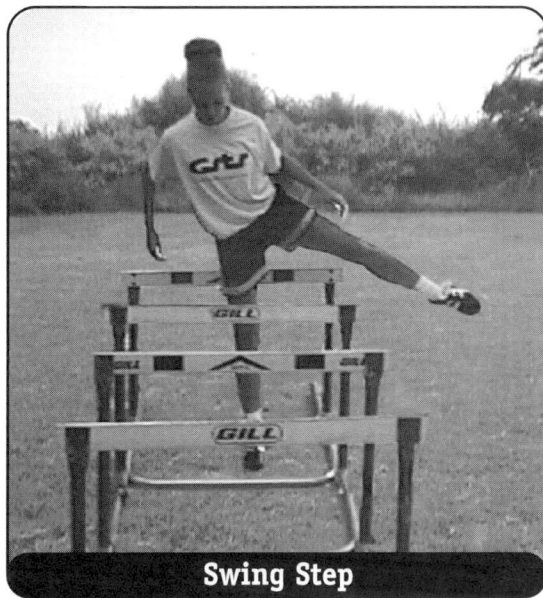

Swing Step

To improve hip mobility this routine should be done both before workout as part of the warm-up and after the workout as part of the cooldown. *See photos.*

Over the Top
Emphasize abducting knee up to the armpit and then bringing the knee to the mid line.

Swing Step
Swing the leg out and around and over the hurdle. Follow immediately with the opposite leg.

Over/Under
Step over one hurdle and crouch under the next hurdle set at a higher height. Especially important for goalkeeper.

Over/Under

BIG KICK ROUTINE

Pawing — *see photo*
Reach out with the foreleg and paw back.

Abduction — *see photo*
From the midline move the leg away from the midline. Return to the midline under control.

Adduction — *see photo*
Start with the involved leg away from the midline and move leg across the midline.

Kicks — *see photo*
  a) From balance position on one leg.
  b) With a step.

Adduction

Pawing

Abduction

Kicks

BALANCE ROUTINE

Single Leg Squat* — *see photos*
(Hold each position ten counts)
  a) *Straight Ahead* — two x each leg
  b) *Side* — two x each leg
  c) *Rotation* — two x each leg

Balance Shift*
(Hold each position six to ten counts)
Shift from the center. The upper body should be quiet.

  a) Shift right on to right leg
  b) Shift left on to left leg
  c) Step forward on to right leg
  d) Step forward on to left leg
  e) Step back on to right leg
  f) Step back on to left leg

Once the player is proficient at balancing, add the ball so that the player works the ball with the free leg. — see photos

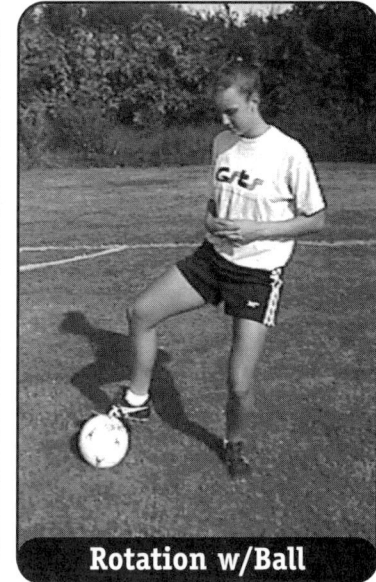

a) Straight Ahead

b) Side

c) Rotation

Straight Ahead w/Ball

Side w/Ball

Rotation w/Ball

ACCELERATION TEACHING PROGRESSION

To teach, analyze and train speed, use the PAL method. PAL is an acronym for POSTURE, ARM ACTION and LEG ACTION. The intention is to teach and analyze movement in that order.

POSTURE

All movement is initiated from the center of the body. This will result in a line of force — **Triple Extension**. Any deviation from this posture (i.e., bending at the waist, dropping or picking up the head) will negatively affect the application of force against the ground.

Soccer Start — *see photos, opposite page*
Feet slightly wider than hip width apart; Knees slightly bent; Shoulders over the knees; Hands held relaxed at about waist level.

Soccer Start Fall And Walk Out
Using the soccer start position; walk out for five steps. The steps should be short and quiet. Steps that are too long will result in a slapping sound against the ground.

Soccer Start Fall And Jog Out
Use the soccer start position, jog out for five steps. Each step should be slightly longer than the previous step.

Soccer Start - Fall And Catch Partner
— *see photo, opposite page*
Lean from the center. Partner catches with the hands on the front of the shoulders. Hold for five counts to get the player to feel the lean from the ankles and alignment of the body.

Soccer Start - Lean/Fall/Run
— *see photo, opposite page*
Put it all together into a smooth pattern of acceleration for eight to ten steps. Fall from the center and sprint out.

Triple Extension

Soccer Start

Soccer Start - Fall And Catch Partner

Soccer Start side view

Soccer Start - Lean/Fall/Run

ARM ACTION

Giant Swing - Big To Little — *see photo*
Begin swinging the arms from the shoulder and gradually bend the elbows until there is a normal sprint arm action. Emphasize swinging from the shoulders.

Seated Arm Action — *see photo*
In a seated position with the legs extended, execute a sprinting arm action emphasizing hammer action down and back. See a hand in front of the chest at all times. Scrape the knuckles on the grass. Be sure to stay relaxed through the shoulders.

Standing Arm Action - Exchange Drill
— *see photos*
Start with one hand at chin level, and the other hand in line with the opposite hip. On the command of switch, change position of the hands with an emphasis on driving the arm down and back. See a hand in front of the chest at all times.

Soccer Start - Lean/Fall/Run
Focus on integration of correct arm action into the whole movement.

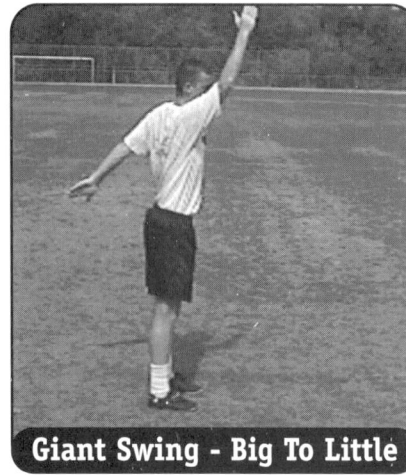

Giant Swing - Big To Little

Seated Arm Action

Standing Arm Action - Exchange Drill

LEG ACTION

Push - Push Drill

Use the soccer start position with a partner. The partner gives heavy resistance with hands on the front of the shoulders. Resist for six steps to force triple extension of ankle/knee/hip.

Contrast Drill

The partner gives heavy resistance for three steps, then gradually reduces resistance over the next three steps until there is no resistance; then release, turns, and runs, forcing the partner to catch up. This will force the player to apply force correctly back against the ground, and to feel the correct pattern of acceleration.

Soccer Start - Drop And Go — *see photo*

The partner applies support by putting both hands on the players shoulders. Get them leaning out as far as possible. This will teach the resisted player to initiate movement from the center, as well as get the foot down to create a positive shin angle. This is a very good first step quickness drill.

Knee Hugs — *see photo*

Pull the knee to the chest and hold that position until you get full extension off the supporting/driving leg. This will create separation between the two legs resulting in a more efficient, pushing leg action.

Knee Hug Drop And Go — *see photo*

The partner applies support by putting both hands on the players shoulders. Initiate movement by leaning forward from the center. Partner then releases the pressure and the player must get the foot down to create a positive shin angle and be in a position to run out.

Soccer Start - Lean/Fall/Run

Always finish with the whole action to integrate all components into the whole.

Knee Hugs

Soccer Start - Drop And Go

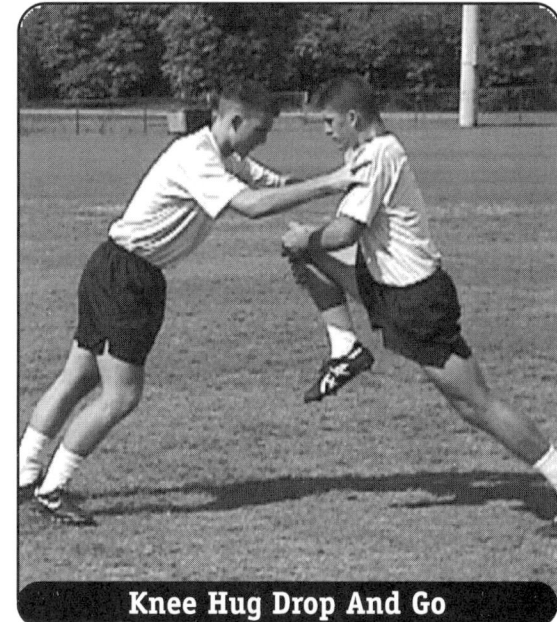
Knee Hug Drop And Go

STRAIGHT AHEAD SPEED DRILLS {ACCELERATION}

START

The goal is to recreate every possible starting scenario that could occur in the course of a game or practice.

Stationary Start — *see photo*

a) Soccer Start - Parallel Stance (used primarily for teaching correct mechanics). In soccer, seldom should movement begin from a standing start. Use a hoop to regulate placement of the first step.

b) Staggered Stance (both right and left foot forward) - To teach pushing off of one foot and getting the back foot down to create a positive shin angle. It is most common in soccer to start with one foot or the other forward while moving.

Walking Start — *see illustration*

From a walking start, hit a mark (a line) with the right foot, and accelerate off that foot. Repeat with the left foot.

Running Start — *see illustration*

From a running start, hit a mark (a line) with the right foot, and accelerate off that foot. Repeat with the left foot.

Downhill Start

Use a slight downhill to overcome inertia. The downhill will also force the player to get the feet down quickly which helps eliminate excessively long steps. The incline facilitates a positive shin angle.

Dancing Start

(Pay particular attention that the first step is in the intended direction. Do not allow the player to false-step.)

Begin with both feet moving.

a) Without Reaction

Start off the right foot (the first step is with the left foot).

Start off the left foot (the first step is with the right foot).

b) With Reaction

React to a clap, a ball, teammate, or opponent.

Sidestep & Go

Off the right and left foot.

a) Take two steps sideways and opposite to the direction of the run; then drive off the back foot and accelerate out for ten yards.

Stationary Start

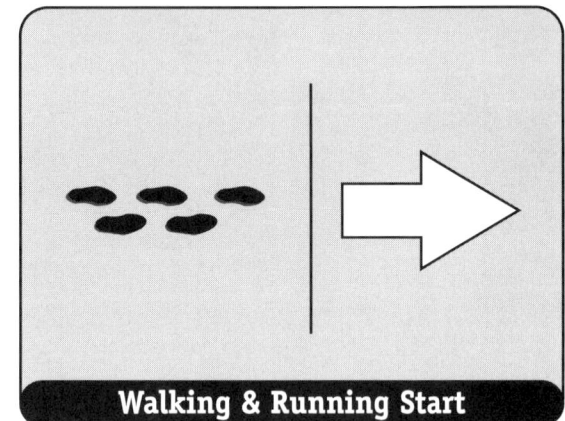
Walking & Running Start

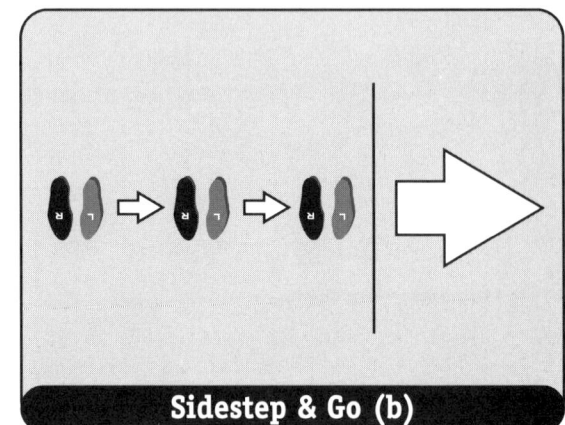
Sidestep & Go (b)

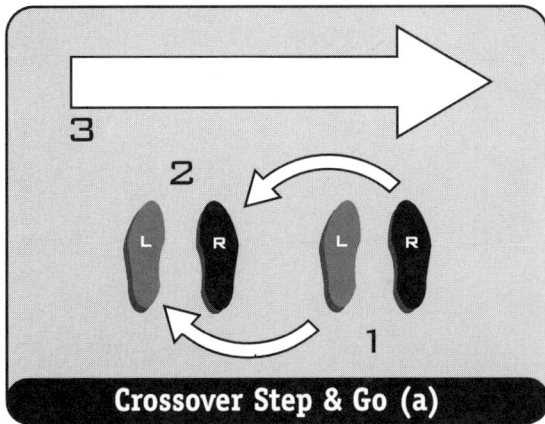
Crossover Step & Go (a)

Scramble Out (a)

Jump & Go

Scramble Out (b)

Jump & Go

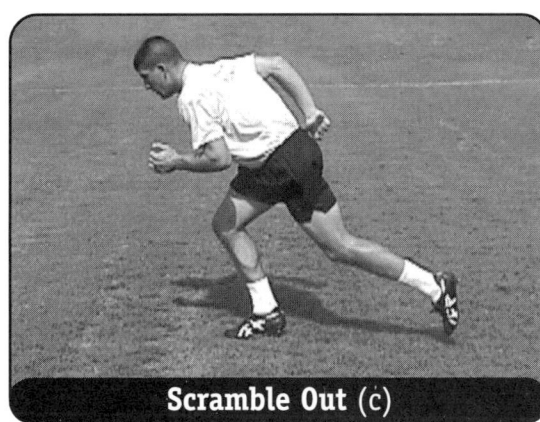
Scramble Out (c)

b) Take two steps sideways in the direction of the run, then drive off the front foot and accelerate out for ten yards.

Crossover Step & Go — *see illustration*

Crossover with the back foot and drive off the front foot. Execute with both a right and left crossover.

a) Execute both a right and left crossover opposite to the intended direction.

b) Execute both a right and left crossover in the same direction.

Jump & Go — *see photo*

Jump off two legs onto one leg, explode off the landing leg and accelerate out. Execute both off the right and left foot. Accelerate out for ten yards.

Scramble Out (Start prone position)
— *see photos*

Start in a prone position with the hands placed near the shoulders. From this position scramble out and accelerate for ten yards.

Seat Roll & Go

Start in a front support position on hands and feet; drop to the butt and roll with the only point of contact the buttocks. After the roll is completed, scramble out and sprint ten yards. This is to teach the player to roll after a fall and get up and run.

Forward Roll & Go

Start in a front support position on hands and feet; execute a forward roll and scramble up into a sprint.

Drop Step & Go

Start facing the opposite direction of the intended sprint. Drop the foot back on the side of the intended sprint. Drive the opposite arm forward and sprint out.

180 Jump & Go — *see photo*

Start facing the opposite direction of the intended run. Jump off both feet turning a 180 in the air, and land and accelerate ten yards.

Plant & Drive Off — *see photos*

Plant the right foot and drive diagonally to the left. Plant the left foot and drive diagonally to the right.
  a) Standing Start
  b) Dancing Start
  c) Running Start

Push & Go — *see photo*

Partner pushes against the hip. Go *with* pressure, or *away* from pressure.

Shoulder Bump & Go

Two players line up side by side about one yard apart. Jump up at the same time and hit at shoulder; regain balance, land, and sprint out.

Push & Go

180 Jump & Go

Plant & Drive Off

Plant & Drive Off

Slide Tackle Start

Slide Tackle Start

Slide Tackle Start

Low Box Starts (a)

Low Box Starts (b)

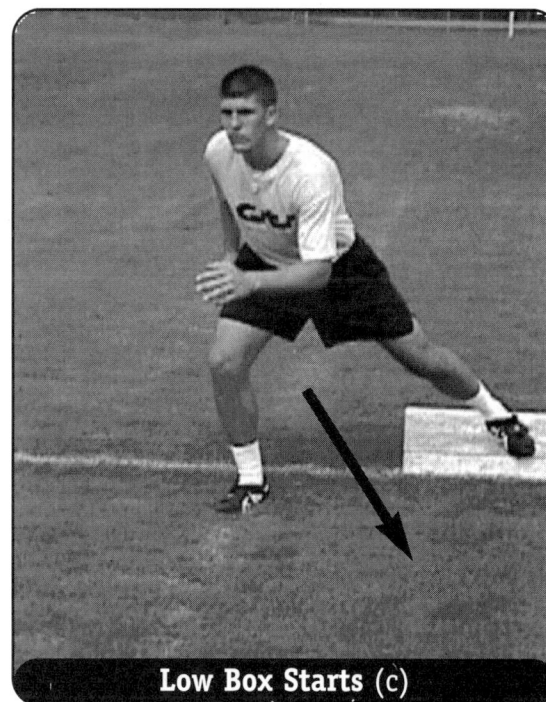

Low Box Starts (c)

Slide Tackle Start — *see photos*
  a) Start with one side lying on the ground and roll forward and up.
  b) Execute a slide tackle; roll forward and go.

Low Box Starts — *see photos*
(The box should be four inches high and twenty four inches square).
  a) Start on the box; and sprint off.
  b) Run onto the box and sprint off - right & left foot.
  c) Run onto the box; plant and drive off right & left foot.

Seated Start

Start seated facing away from the intended direction of the sprint; stand up, turn and sprint for ten yards.

Stick Drill — *see illustration*

(Drill to teach the proper pattern of acceleration): Accelerate from a standing start and hit a series of sticks placed at distances that increase in length with each step. The spacing of the sticks determines the pattern of acceleration. (It is also possible to use hoops to accomplish the same patterning of the acceleration.) You will need to experiment with the spacing based on the leg length and developmental level of the player. A good starting point is to place the second stick thirty centimeters from the first and increase the distance between each stick proportionately by fifteen centimeter increments so the spacing would be 15 cm, 30 cm, 45 cm, 60 cm etc. The soccer player should use five or six sticks. Be sure that the athlete is applying force back against the sticks. Use this drill as a teaching aid to reinforce good mechanics; be careful not to overuse it.

Stick Drill

STRAIGHT AHEAD SPEED DRILLS
{DECISION-MAKING SPEED}

Decision Making Start - React to movement

a) Moving in place - Move in the opposite or in the same direction of a partner who initiates the movement.

b) Moving forward- Move in the opposite or in the same direction of a partner who initiates the movement.

Low Five

Sprint out to a partner who is holding a hand at knee height and touch the hand.

Give and Go — *see illustration*

Player A passes the ball to player B and sprints forward.

Give-Go-Get — *see illustration*

Player A passes the ball to player B and sprints forward. Player B gives player A return pass. Player A receives the ball on the run and continues with a speed dribble. To challenge the player place cones ten yards apart and time player for that segment both with and without the ball.

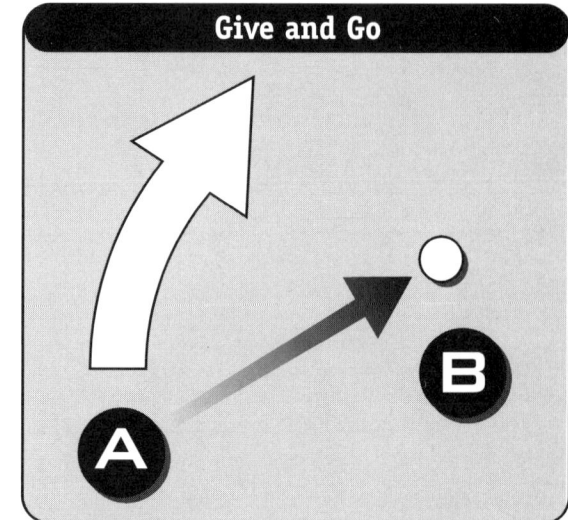

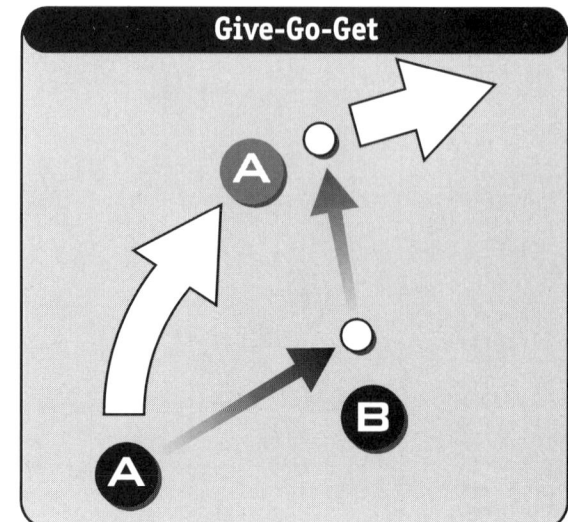

Give and Go

Give-Go-Get

Give-Go-Get & Turn — *see illustration*

Player A passes the ball to player B and sprints forward. Player B gives player A return pass. Player A receives the ball and turns with the ball to reverse direction.

Numbered Cones — *see photo*

Start sprinting straight ahead. A coach or partner calls out the number of a cone to run around and return to the staring position. It is best performed by two players to insure proper recovery between runs.

Give-Go-Get & Turn

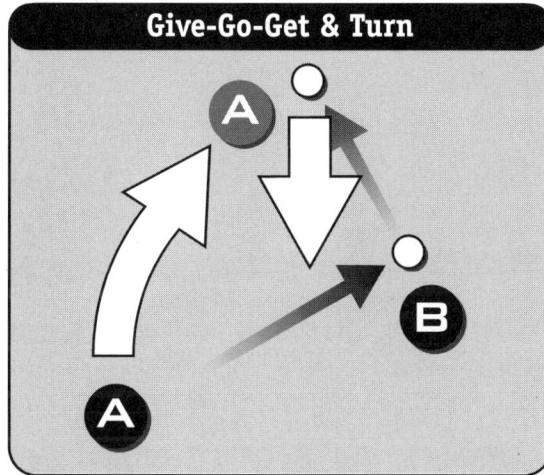

Numbered Cones

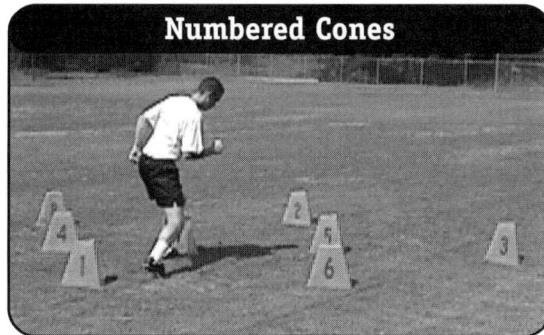

STRAIGHT AHEAD SPEED DRILLS
{SPEED IN COOPERATION}

Two Player Serpentine — *see illustration*

Player A and B start out running parallel to each other with about five yards spacing. Player A will run in a serpentine fashion while player B follows player A's lead.

Two Player Weave — *see illustration*

Two lines of players. Line one leads and initiates the action. Line two follows. The player leading always crosses in front.

Two Player Serpentine

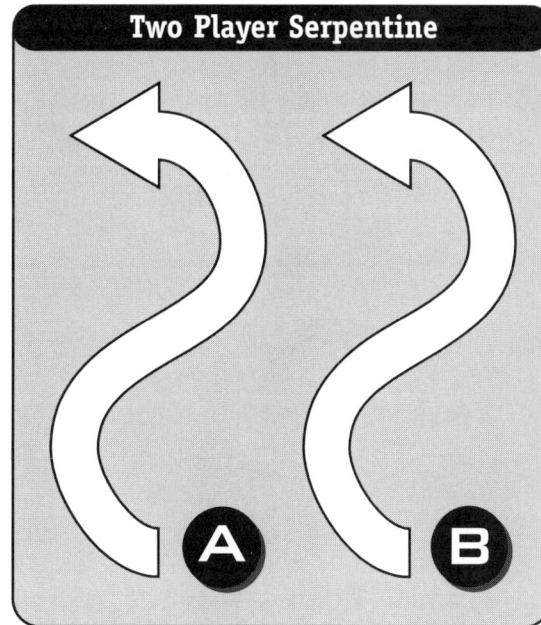

Two Player Weave

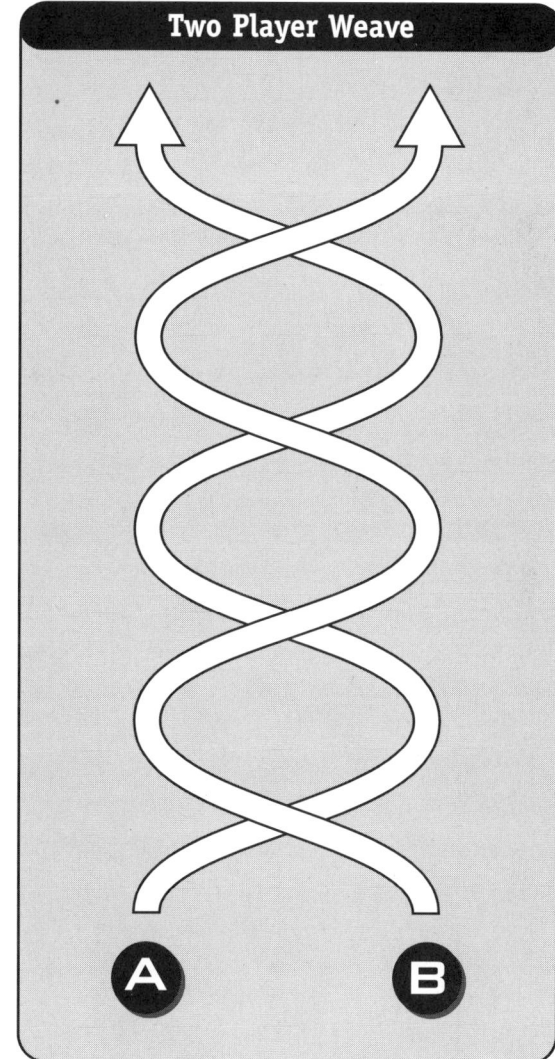

Three Player Weave — *see illustration*
Always cross in front. Number the players in three lines. The first action is initiated by one, then two, then three. Each line takes a turn at leading and initiating the action which results in three rotations.

Single File Weave — *see illustration*
With a line of at least five players running at a spacing of double arms distance apart. The last player in the line weaves forward through the teammates. When that player reaches the front of the line the next player weaves forward. Go once through the group then jog for two minutes.

Speed In Cooperation (Partners)
 a) Touching - Hand on hip of partner. Stay in touching distance throughout the sprint. — *see illustration*
 b) Mirror - Follow one step behind the leader. Mirror the leaders movements. — *see illustration*

Two Person Follow The Leader
 a) Same Direction
The following player moves in the same direction as the leader.
 b) Opposite direction
The following player moves in the opposite direction as the leader.

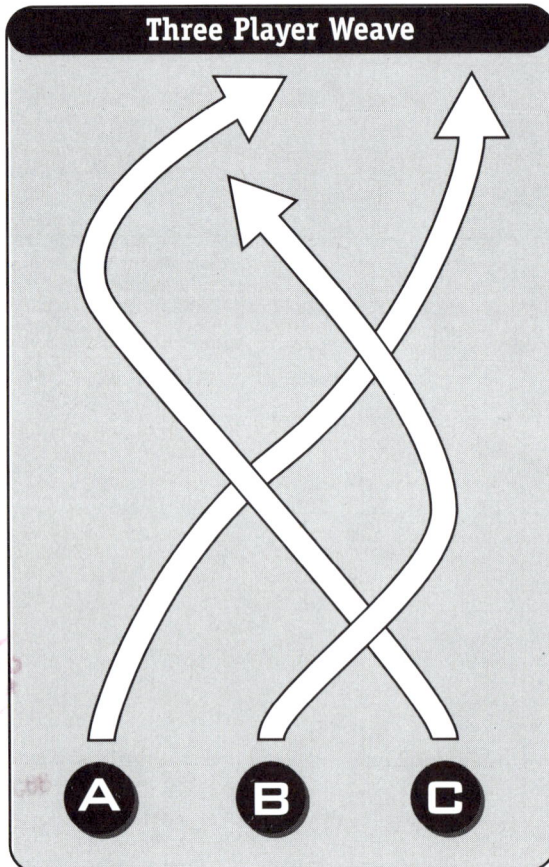

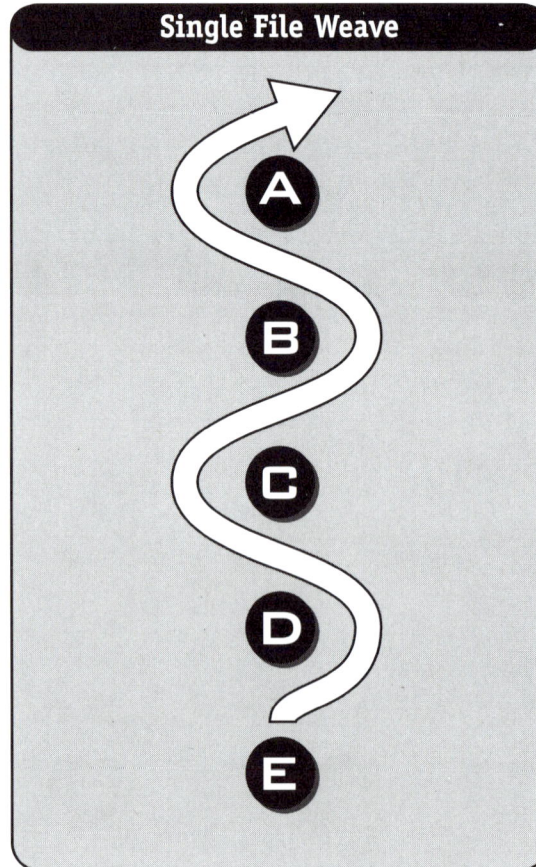

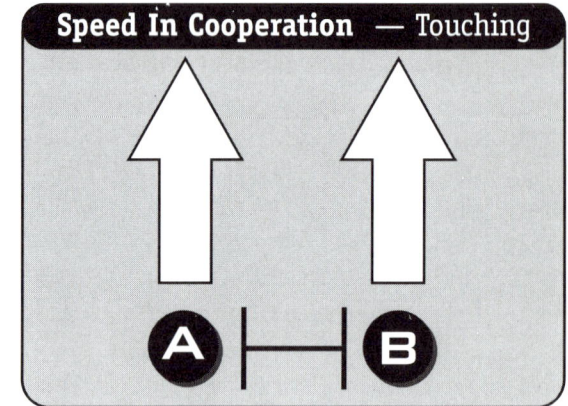

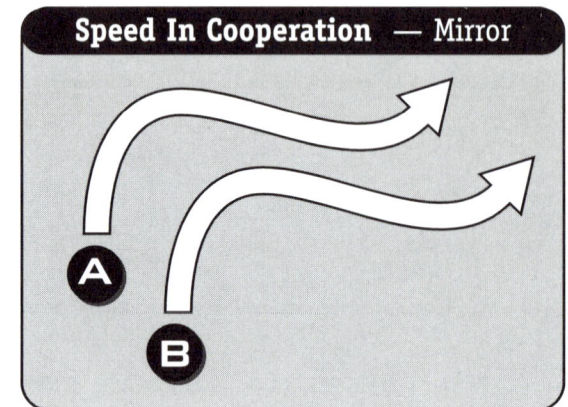

Three Player Weave

Single File Weave

Speed In Cooperation — Touching

Speed In Cooperation — Mirror

STRAIGHT AHEAD SPEED DRILLS
{RESISTANCE}

Two Hops & Sprint — *see illustration*
Execute two hops on right or left foot then sprint.

Four Bounds Into Sprint — *see illustration*
Start off the right foot and execute four bounds: right/left/right/left into a sprint. Repeat off the left foot: left/right/left/ right into a sprint.

Harness Runs — *see photo*
Use the "overload" of the harness to facilitate good posture. Use just enough resistance so that the athlete can feel the extension and pushing action against the ground. Too much resistance will slow the action and alter the mechanics of acceleration. A good variation is to release the harness after five or seven steps to create a contrast effect. This also serves to test the athlete's posture and overall mechanics. Everything is mechanically sound if the transition at the point of release is smooth.

Sled or Tire Pull — *see photo*
Use the sled to overload. Observe the 10% rule: The resistance of the sled should not slow the runner down more than 10% of the best time of the distance being run nor should the resistance exceed 10% of the athletes bodyweight.

Contrast Harness
Twenty yards - Heavy resistance for ten yards then light resistance for ten yards.

Four Bounds Into Sprint

Harness Runs

Sled or Tire Pull

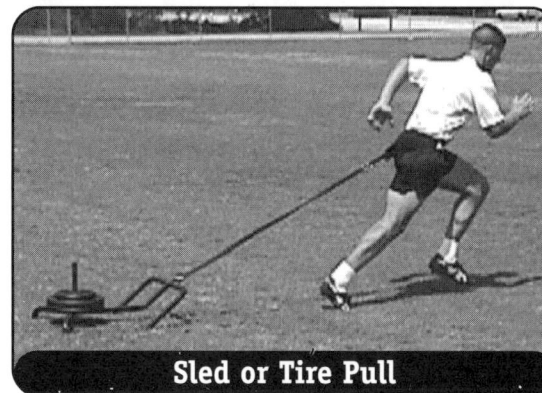
Two Hops & Sprint

Hill Sprints

Use a hill with an incline of approximately 40-45 degrees. The length should be 50 to 100 yards in length. The hill will develop push-off and stride frequency.

Parachute

Throw the parachute up and behind when starting or have a partner hold the chute up so that the chute is filled with air at the start.

a) Forward Run – The chute is attached behind the player. Even though the wind will cause the chute to move around the player should run straight ahead.

— *see photo*

b) Backward – The chute is attached in front of the player so that the player backpedals with the chute as resistance. As the chute moves around with the wind the player should move with the chute as if guarding the chute — *see photo*

c) Weave – The chute is attached behind the player. The player runs in a weaving pattern.

Sand

Sprint in sand. Use both standing and moving starts. The distance of the sprint should be between twenty and thirty yards.

Contrast

Sand to Grass - Start so that the first five steps are in sand, then onto grass for five steps.

Uphill to level - Start so that the first ten steps are uphill, then crest the hill and sprint ten steps on level ground.

Downhill to level - Start so that the first ten steps are downhill, onto level ground, then continue the sprint for ten steps.

Parachute a) Forward

Parachute b) Backward

STRAIGHT AHEAD SPEED DRILLS
{ASSISTANCE}

Towing — *see illustration*

The key is not to tow the player faster than they are capable of running, but to get them to run relaxed and work on good top speed mechanics. It is preferable to use a pulley device because of the smooth nature of the pull as well as safety considerations.

a) Short Pull – Pull hard for five to eight strides and then release the pull so that the player runs on their own.

b) Long Pull – Pull for twenty to thirty yards.

Downhill

Use a 2-3% downhill grade. Downhill sprinting will improve stride length as well as stride turn over. The distance should be 30 to 50 yards in length.

Flying Sprint

Build up to top speed using a 20 yard distance. The top speed distance should be 10 to 30 yards in length. The emphasis is on running tall and relaxation.

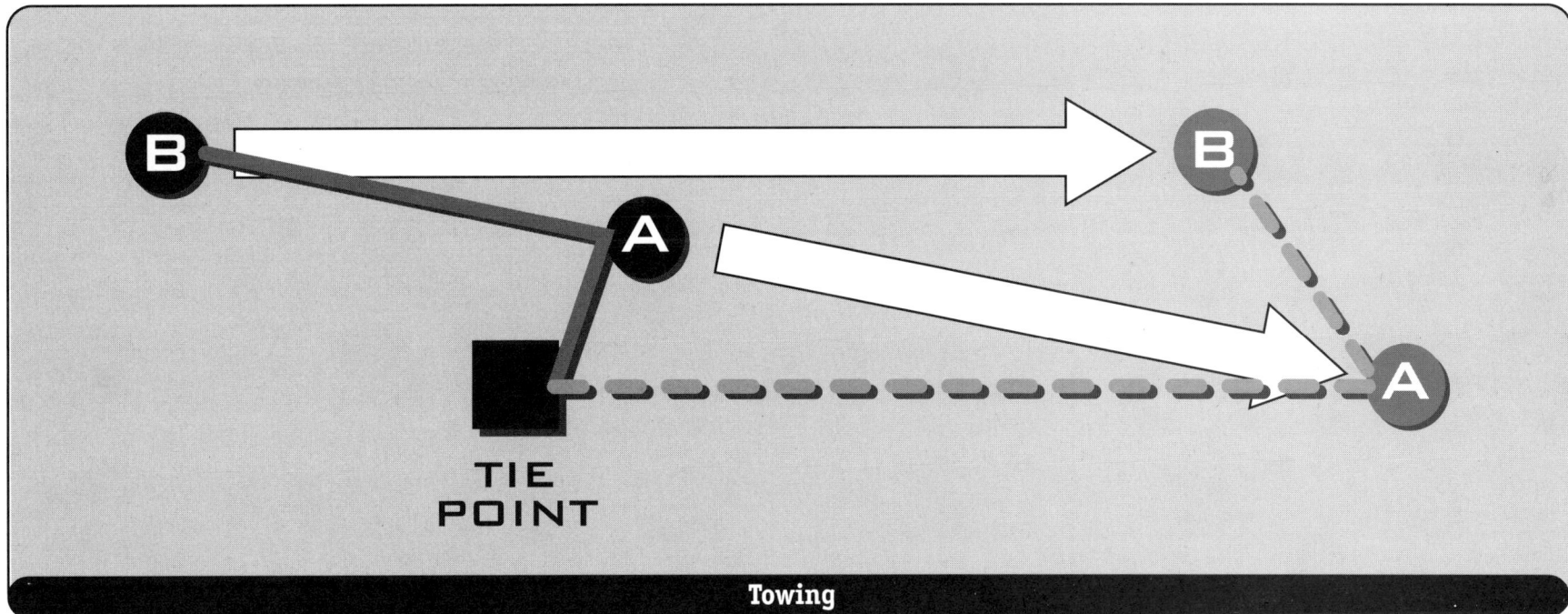

TIE POINT

B

A

B

A

Towing

THE CONCEPT OF LATERAL SPEED AND AGILITY (LSA)

This is the ability to recognize and react to the proper stimulus, start quickly, move in the correct direction, change direction if necessary and stop quickly to make the play.

LSA Training will:
1) Improve quickness on and off the ball
2) Improve body control through control of center of gravity
3) Prevent injury through proper movement mechanics.

The Wheel Principle

KEY CONCEPTS:

The Wheel Principle is the basis for the development of LSA. A great player must be able to move effectively in all spokes of the wheel.

- Starting is extension of the ankle, knee, and hip.
- Stopping is flexion (bending) of the ankle, knee, and hip.
- Change of direction requires control of the center of gravity in all planes and all directions.
- "Game Speed" is control of the speed that is required to make the play.

FOOTWORK

The objective of proper footwork is to gain a step. The most common footwork error is the false step. This occurs when the player steps back before stepping forward or otherwise steps away from the intended direction of movement.

The type of step is determined by the distance of the required movement:

Crossover Power Step

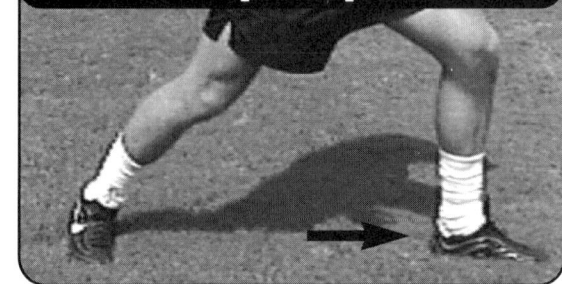

Open Step

Jab Step

Drop Step

Crossover Power Step — *see photo*

This is appropriate when the distance to be moved is relatively great. The lead foot remains stationary and the back foot crosses over in front of the lead foot. The push-off is from the lead foot.

Open Step — *see photo*

This is appropriate when the distance to be moved is short, or a quick reaction is required. The lead foot steps out with the push-off from the back foot. The situation will determine when, or if, you use this step.

Jab Step — *see photo*

Also can be used when the distance is short and a quick reaction is required. This is a movement backward of the lead foot relative to the center of gravity. The situation will determine when or if you use this step.

Drop Step — *see photo*

Used when it is necessary to move back either diagonally or straight back. The lead foot moves back diagonally or straight back. The push-off is from the back foot.

LSA TEACHING/TRAINING PROGRESSION

Use this progression when selecting a sequence of exercises.

Step # 1 - Basic Skill

Begin with the most basic movement. Master this movement by emphasizing precision and exact technique in order to form a sound movement pattern.

Step # 2 - Basic Skill with variation

Add complexity by adding a variation to, then master the movement with the variation.

Step # 3 - Basic Skill with reaction

Add reaction, but do not compromise correct movements.

Step # 4 - Basic Skill with opponent and/or the ball

Once the previous four steps have been mastered add an opponent or the ball. This is the actual soccer activity.

SELECTING DRILLS AND EXERCISES:

Separate the need to do from the nice to do. If the drill does not relate, then do not use it. A few drills well chosen, done with speed and correct technique will pay more dividends than a large number of drills done poorly.

Carefully consider the demands of the position. Each position and player require different movement patterns, therefore, it is important to make the drills position specific.

WHEN TO TRAIN LSA

The best time is at beginning of practice or even as part of the warm-up when the players are fresh and better able to assimilate movements.

Once the drills are mastered it is also good to incorporate LSA work during practice mixed with appropriate skill and tactical work. This should be low volume, high intensity work.

After practice is the least desirable place to work this quality. Fatigue will compromise skill learning and speed development.

DETERMINING WORKLOAD

Volume should be determined from game analysis based on the number of the various types of movement that occur in a game.

Intensity should be at "Game Speed" unless a new skill is being learned.

Work : Rest Ratio should be sufficient to insure quality of movement. Once the skill is mastered then it is appropriate to incorporate fatigue. In general the ratio should be 1:2 or 1:3.

Ball Drop One Ball

Ball Drop Two Ball

Z Ball

LATERAL SPEED & AGILITY - REACTION/ RECOGNITION

Ball Drop

The partner drops the ball from head height. The person executing the drill must react and control the ball before the second bounce. Make the drill more difficult by lowering the distance of the drop or moving farther away.

   a) One Ball — *see photo*
   b) Two Ball — *see photo*

This forces the player to react and choose.

Z Ball — *see photo*

Great for reaction training with the goal keeper. This is a small rubber ball with round protrusions that cause the ball to take unpredictable bounces. A keeper can work solo against a wall or with a partner.

Ball Roll

Roll the ball toward a line on the field. When the ball hits the line the player reacts and sprints to the ball.

Recognition Hoops — *see photo*

Use different size or different color hoops to determine footwork. A larger hoop indicates two feet in the hoop. A smaller hoop indicates one foot in the hoop.

Recognition Hoops

Reaction Belt

This a drill using a belt that is attached to each partner with a velcro attachment. One partner is designated as the leader and the other as the follower. The follower tries to stay with the leader mimicking the same movements. The drill ends when the velcro attachment is broken.

Reaction Runs — *see illustrations*

One partner is the leader and the other partner reacts.

a) The partner reacts and moves in the same direction as the leader.

b) The partner reacts and moves in the opposite direction as the leader.

Wave Drill — *see illustration*

Line up five or six players. The first player starts, each player reacts to the movement of the player in front of them.

Reaction Runs (a)

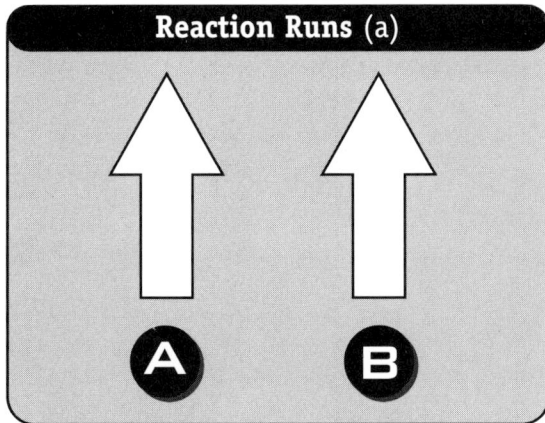

Reaction Runs (b)

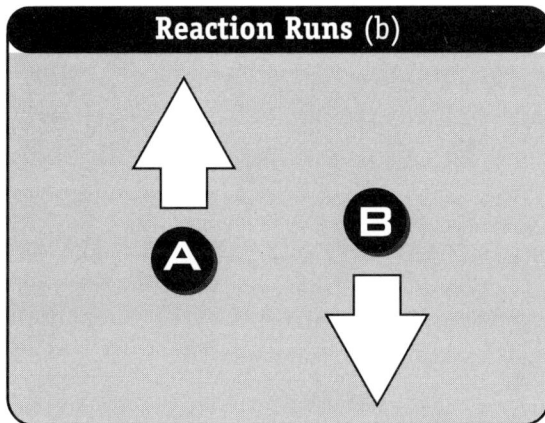

Wave Drill

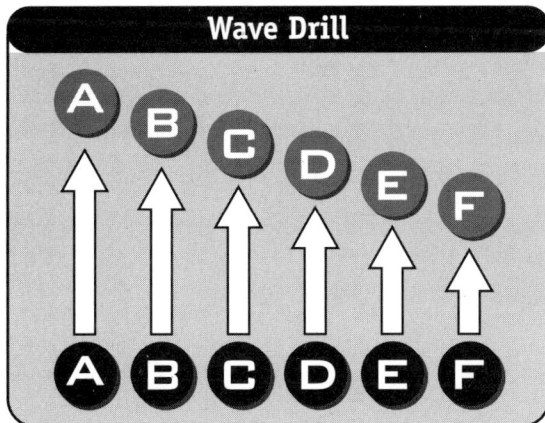

Double Leg Jumps

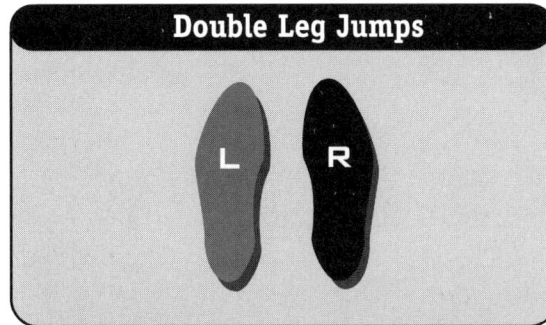

Stride Jumps

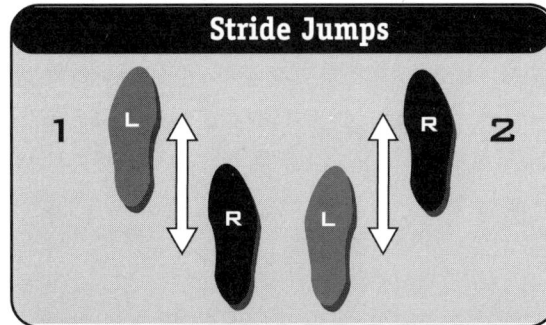

Crossover Jumps

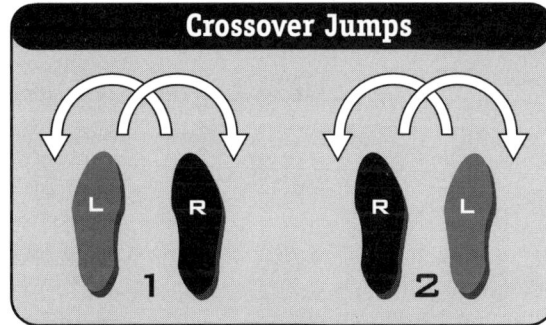

Single Leg Hops

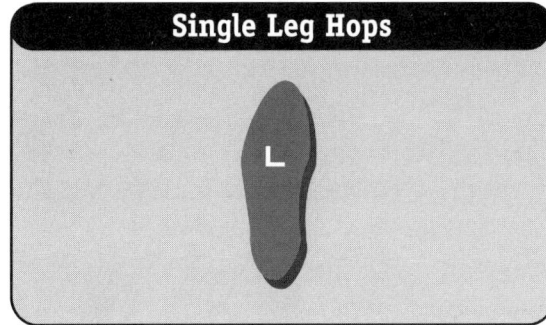

Jump Rope

Jumping rope works hand/foot and hand/eye coordination. It is best to develop a routine that the players can use daily as a warm-up for other footwork drills. The routine is:

a) Double Leg Jumps — *see illustration*
b) Stride Jumps — *see illustration*
c) Crossover Jumps — *see illustration*
d) Single Leg Hops — *see illustration*

You can do these in a series with a prescribed number of jumps for each exercise or for a set time period for each exercise.

Low Box Quickstep — *see photo*

Use a box four inches in height by thirty inches square. Step on and off the box as quickly as possible. Use low quick steps. Continue the drill until the rhythm falls off. The drills can be done straight ahead, side to side or with a combination of boxes.

Low Box Quickstep

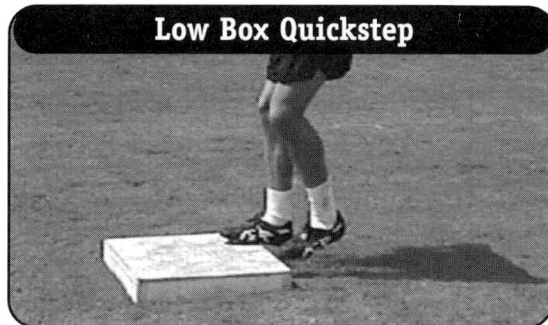

Line Step Over

Start on one side of a line. Step over first with the foot closest to the line and immediately follow with the opposite foot. The idea is to get both feet down as quickly as possible. Immediately repeat back in the opposite direction. The goal is to do the maximum number of reps in ten seconds.

Cone Step Over

Start on one side of a twelve inch cone. Step over first with the foot closest to the cone and immediately follow with the opposite foot. Get both feet down as quickly as possible. Immediately repeat back in the opposite direction. The goal is to do the maximum number of reps in ten seconds.

Hoops Double-In — *see photo*

Using a series of hoops placed in a random pattern, quickly step in and out of each hoop with booth feet.

Hoops Double-In

Speed/Agility Ladder

Control and positioning of the center of gravity is the major objective of proper footwork. This consists of keeping the hips over the base of support if stability is desired, or shifting the center of gravity outside the base of support to initiate movement if a change of direction is necessary.

The first coaching cue is to get your feet back down to the ground. This puts the player in a position to apply force against the ground in order to execute the required move.

Coaching & Observation Points
- Contact point — Preferably toward the ball of the foot.
- Weight distribution — The weight should be distributed over the whole foot to take full advantage of the propulsive forces available.
- Height of step — A low heel recovery is necessary to put the foot in proper position to push against the ground. Movement upward is a wasted motion. The cue is to step over the ankle.
- Sound — Quiet! No slapping or loud noise on foot contact.
- Rhythm/Tempo — The foot contact should be rhythmic. Pretend you are dancing! Use music with the drills to emphasize rhythm.

Remember: let your feet take you to the ball!

Speed/Agility Ladder Basic Series

Descriptions for all the speed ladder exercises were written by Steve Myrland.

Forward One In: Facing the length of the ladder, move quickly through the squares, placing your feel alternatively in each. — *see illustration*

Forward Two In: Facing the length of the ladder, move through the rungs placing both feet in each square. Do the exercise leading with the right foot, then repeat with the left. — *see illustration*

Lateral Two-In: Stand with your shoulders turned parallel to the length of the ladder, and leading with near foot (right shoulder, right foot, for example). Move quickly through all the squares, placing both feet in each. Keep your feet parallel to the rungs of the ladder. Repeat the exercise, leading with the other shoulder and foot. — *see illustration*

Lateral Cross-step: Stand with your shoulders turned parallel to the length of the ladder, and leading with near foot (right shoulder, right foot, for example). Cross your trailing foot over the lead foot and continue down the length of the ladder placing the feet alternately in the squares, continually crossing the trailing foot in front of the leading foot. Keep your feet parallel to the length of the ladder. Repeat the exercise leading with the opposite shoulder and foot. — *see illustration*

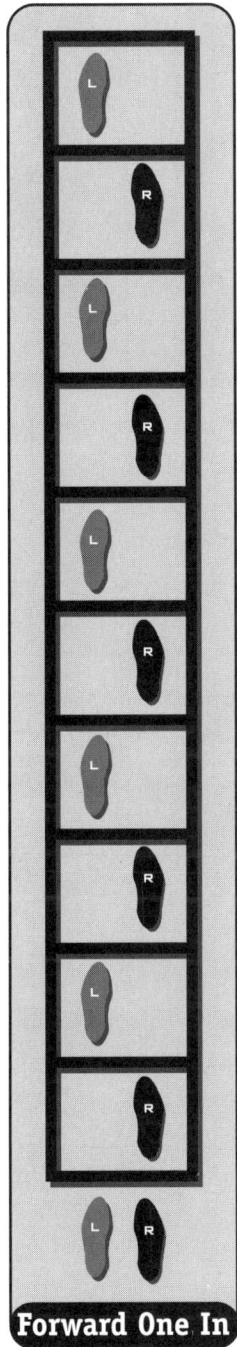

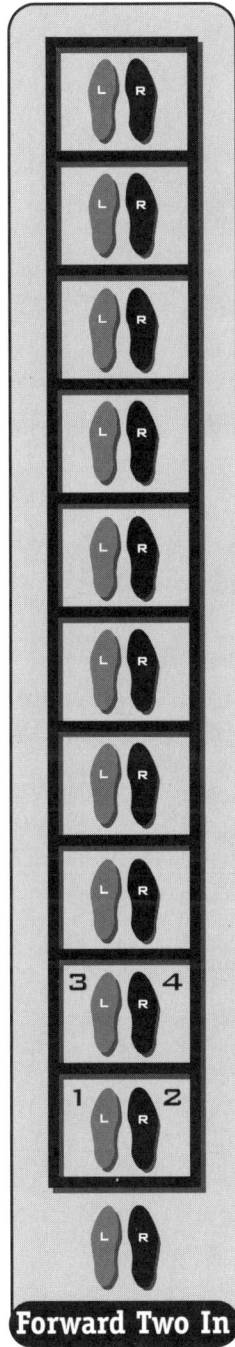

Forward One In   Forward Two In   Lateral Two In   Lateral Cross Step   Ali Shuffle Two In   Ali Shuffle One In

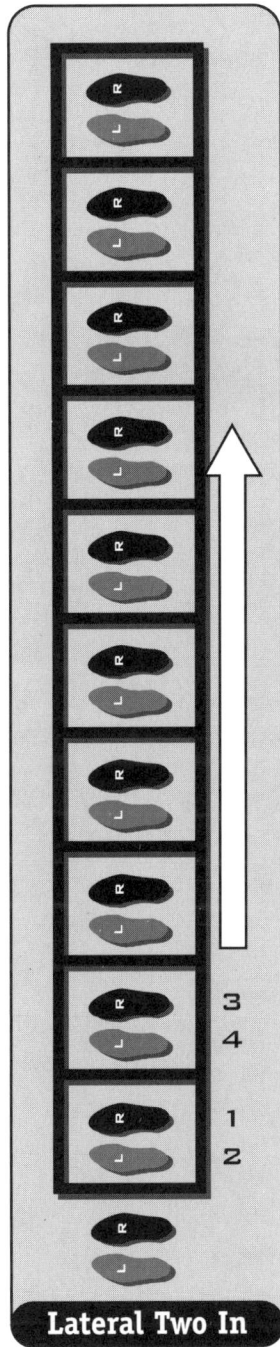

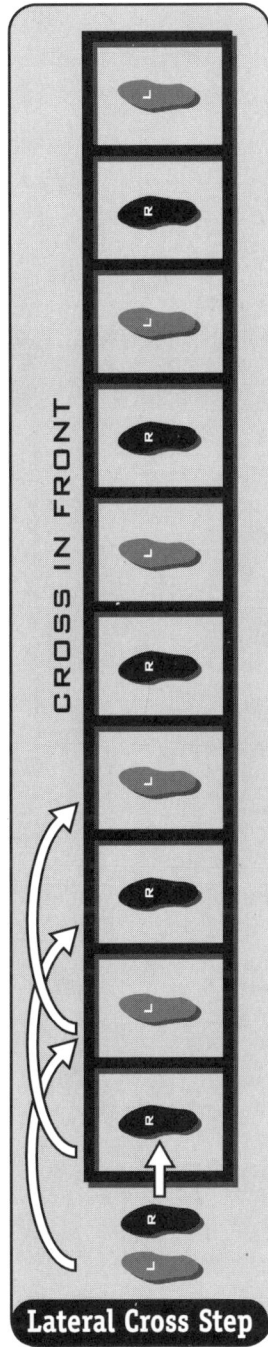

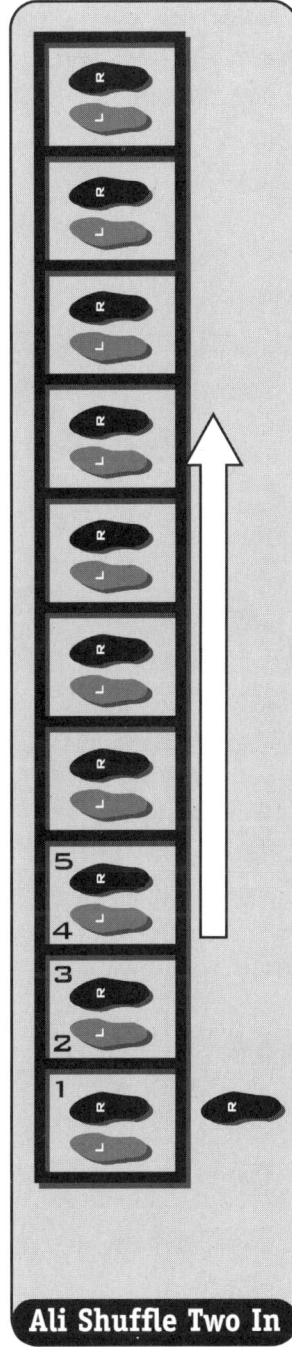

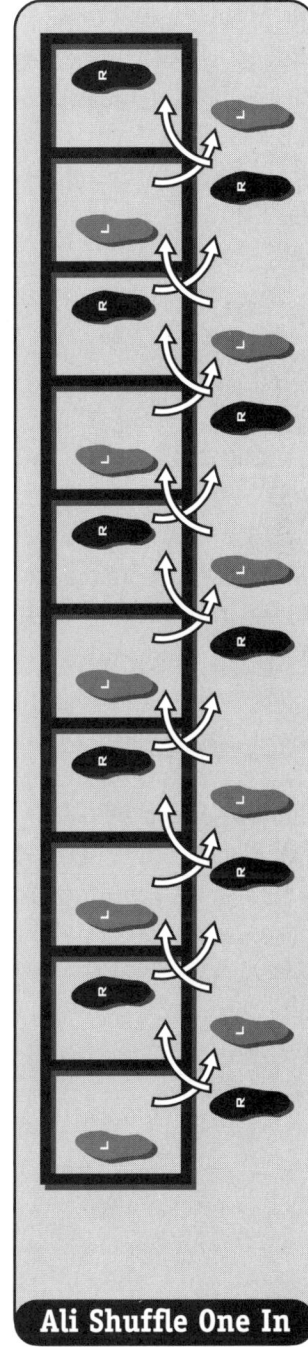

CROSS IN FRONT

39

Ali-Shuffle (Two Feet In): Stand with your left shoulder turned parallel to the length of the ladder. In this drill, you move your arms and legs with a minimum of flexion at the knees and elbows. Begin with your left foot in the first space, and your right foot outside the ladder. Your right arm is forward, left arm back. Now, switch your arms and legs so your right foot is in the same ladder space, and your arms are reversed; repeat the movement, this time moving into the second ladder space. You make your rapid arm and leg changes (with minimal elbow and knee bend) and get both feet into each space as you move down the ladder. Repeat the drill with your right shoulder leading. — *see illustration, previous page*

Ali-Shuffle (One Foot In): This is similar to the previous exercise, but you will be placing one foot (alternately) in each ladder space. Begin with your left foot in the first space (right arm forward, left arm back). Now, quickly switch your arms and legs so that you get your right foot in the second space. This requires you to rotate quickly at your hips to facilitate the lateral movement. Synchronizing your arm and leg movements is critical to getting this drill done. — *see illustration, previous page*

Mini Hurdles (Six Inch) — *see illustrations*
Use the lower hurdle to emphasize getting the feet back down on the ground quickly.
a) Even Rhythm (Drawing of foot pattern) The hurdles are placed in an even distance so that the player takes a consistent number of strides between each hurdle.
b) Broken Rhythm (Drawing of foot pattern) The hurdles are placed in random patterns so that no set number of strides is taken between hurdles.

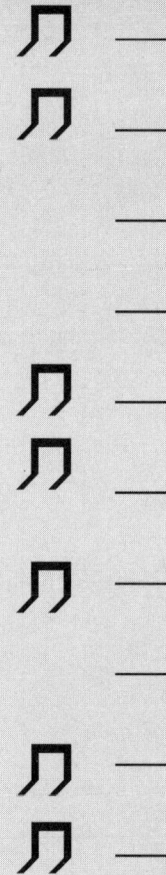

LATERAL SPEED & AGILITY - CHANGE OF DIRECTION

Quarter Eagle — *see photos/illustration*
a) Run Out - Execute a quarter eagle and run out of the end position.
b) Run Out & Return - Execute a quarter eagle and run out of the end position, touch a cone placed five yards away and return to the start.

Scramble Out
a) Run Out - Lying face down with the hands placed at the side of the chest, scramble out as fast as possible.
b) Run Out & Return - Scramble out, touch a cone return as fast as possible to the starting position.

Z Band — *see photo*
Anchor a piece of rubber tubing in a Z

Mini Hurdles
Even Rhythm

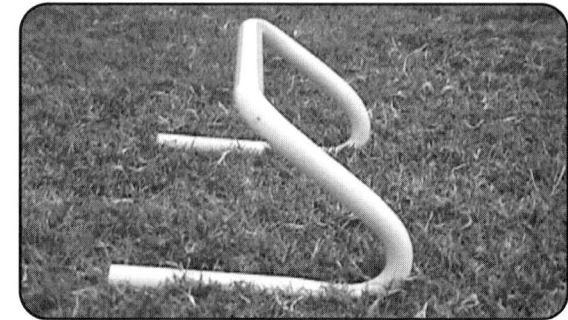

Mini Hurdles
Broken Rhythm

Quarter Eagle (Pos 1)

Pos 2

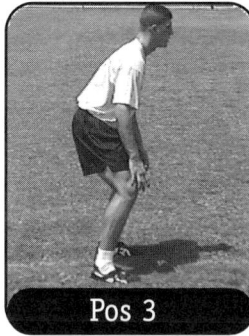

Pos 3

Quarter Eagle

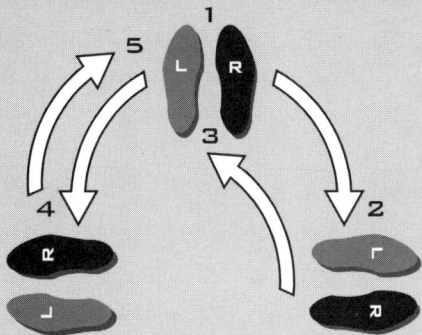

Z Band

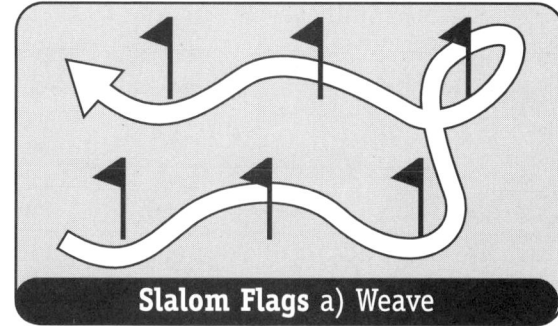

Slalom Flags a) Weave

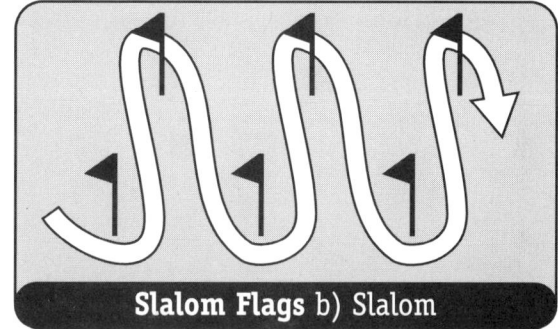

Slalom Flags b) Slalom

pattern so that it is six to eight inches in height.

a) Plant & Cut - Plant and cut at each angle.

b) Plant & Cut & Return - Plant and cut at each angle execute an inside turn and return down the opposite side.

Slalom Flags

Place the flags four to five yards apart.

a) Weave – weave in and out of each flag. — *see illustration*

b) Slalom – run around the outside of the first flag then run across to the flag on the opposite side — *see illustration*

c) Plant & Cut – Plant the outside foot outside of each flag and drive off to the opposite flag. — *see photo*

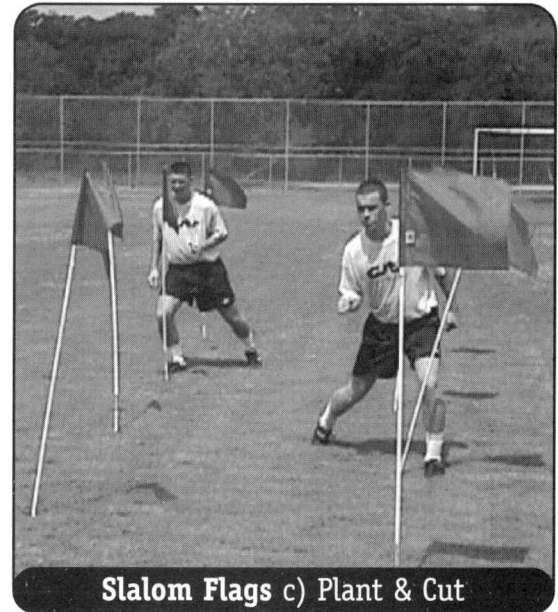

Slalom Flags c) Plant & Cut

d) Plant & Shuffle – Plant the outside foot outside of each flag and shuffle to the opposite flag.

5-10-5 Quick Change — *see illustration*

Execute each movement beginning by moving five yards in one direction. Plant the foot at the end of five yards and change to the opposite direction for ten yards. Then move five yards back in the opposite direction back to the start. Execute each of the following movements starting both to the right and to the left:

a) Shuffle
b) Carioca
c) Back & Forward
d) Side to Side

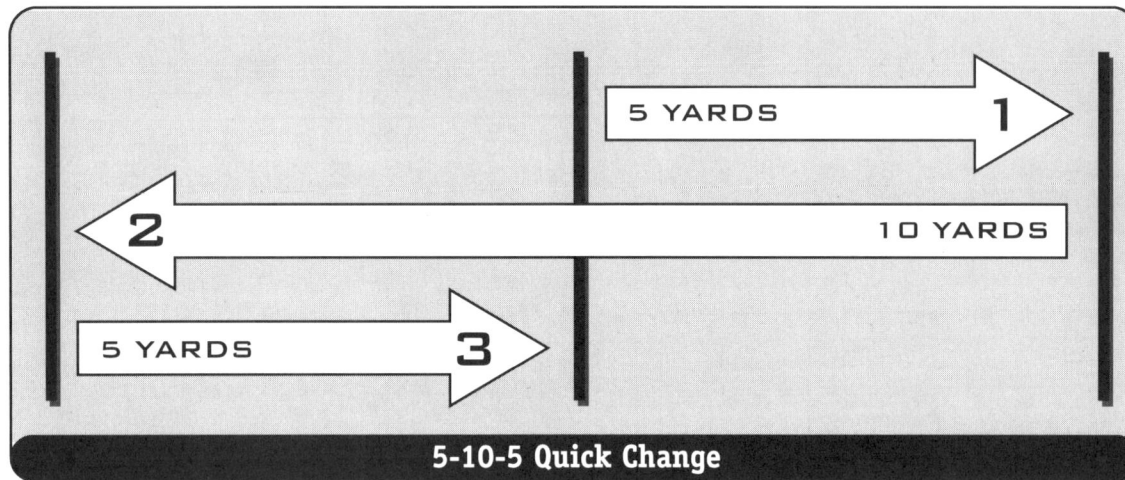

5-10-5 Quick Change

SPEED/AGILITY LADDER CHANGE OF DIRECTION FOOTWORK DRILLS

Three-count Shuffle: Stand to the left of the ladder, facing down its length. Step into the first square with your right foot, then your left foot, then step out to the right side of the ladder with your right foot. Now reverse the steps to the left moving forward to the second square (left foot in, right foot in, left foot out). This is a waltz: 1, 2, 3; 1, 2, 3 and so on. You can learn the exercise best by saying the following words as you go: "in-in-out; in-in-out." Just make sure you begin with the foot nearest the ladder. — *see illustration*

Three-count Cross-Step: Begin in the same position as the Three-count Shuffle, but this time cross your left (outside) foot over your right to land in the first square; then step outside the ladder to the right with your right foot and then your left. Reverse the steps toward the left (right foot in, left foot out, right foot out). This is still a waltz, but your word-cues are as follows: "cross-cross-out, cross-cross-out." Always begin with your outside foot. *see illustration*

Backward Shuffle: It's the rule of the game: whatever you are able to do forwards, you must be able to do backwards. Here is a tip for making it work—angle your hips so the near hip is pointing

Three-Count Shuffle

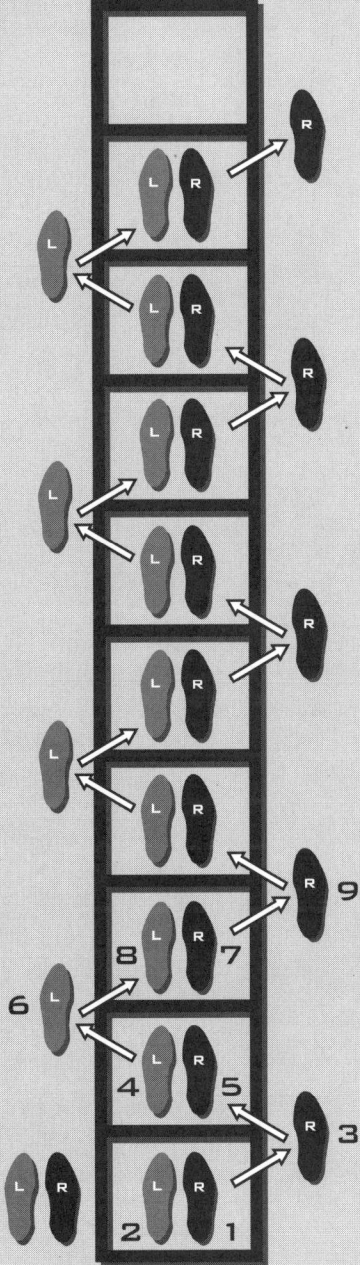

Three-Count Cross-Step:

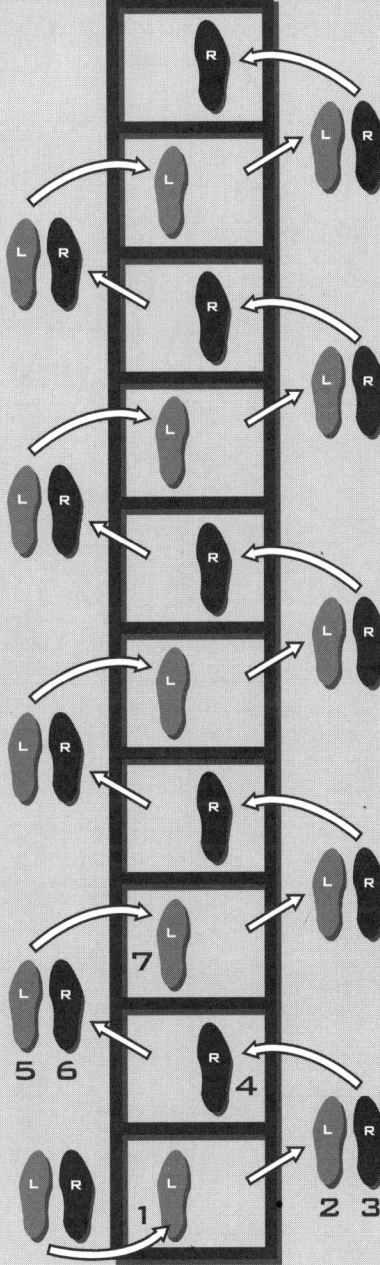

Backward Shuffle

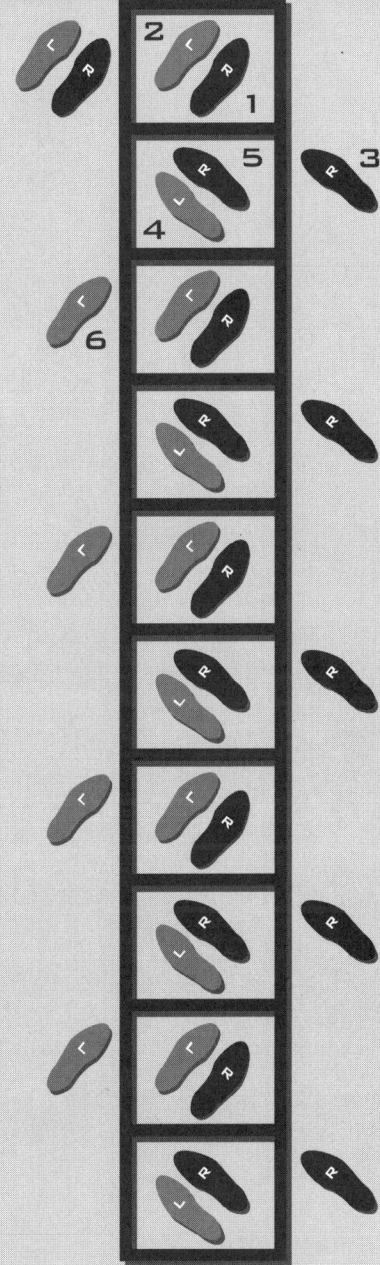

Backward Cross-Step

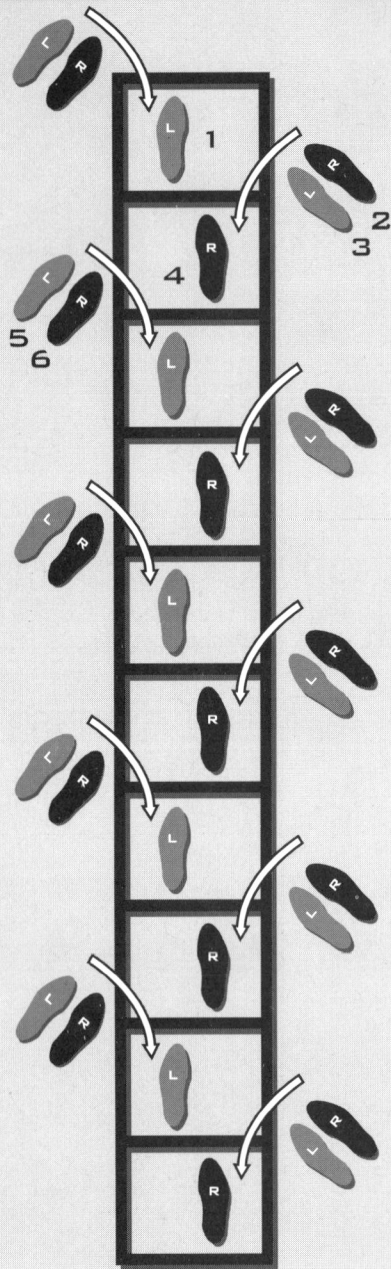

Three-Count Shuffle Bound

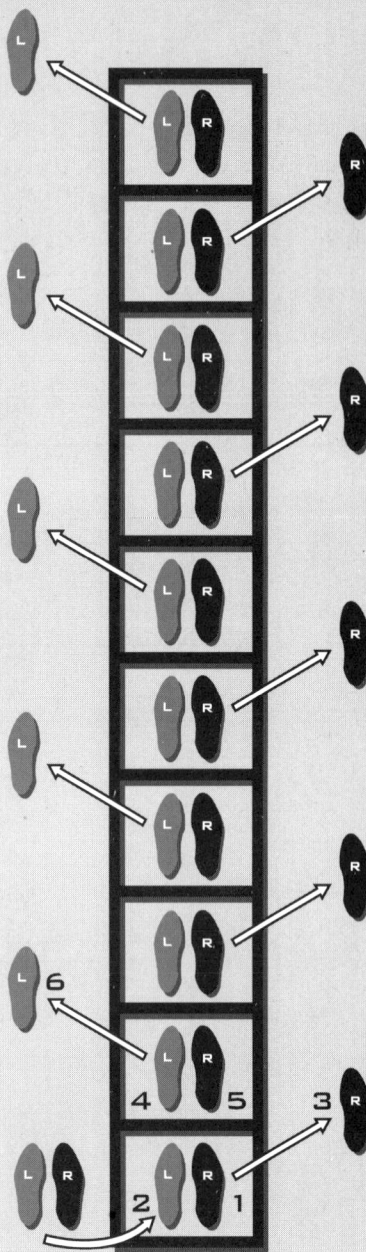

Three-Count Cross Step Bound

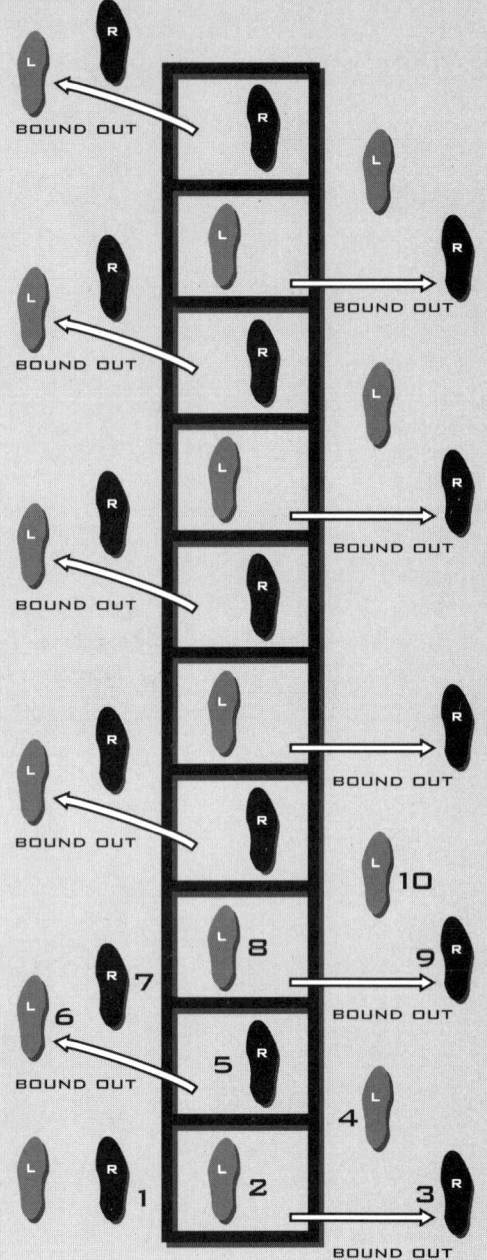

(slightly) down the length of the ladder. In the case of the Three-count Shuffle and the Three-Count Cross-Step, your left hip angles down the ladder when you move back to the right. This mimics the use of the hips in defensive marking and allows you to move without having to look over your shoulder to see where you are going. If you angle your hips correctly, the ladder will simply be there, right where you want it to be. *See illustration, previous page.*

SPEED/AGILITY LADDER PLYOMETRIC COMBINATIONS

Once you have the shuffle and the cross-step down (forwards and backwards) you can add a plyometric component to the exercises and improve your ability to stop, balance, and cut back the other way against increased eccentric loading. In the case of the shuffle, all you do is increase the length of your step as you leave the ladder—(in-in-out), pushing the outside step at least a yard or so beyond the lateral edge of the ladder and the cutting back as quickly as you can to the right. *(see illustration, previous page.)* The increased length of the step forces you to lower your center of gravity as you prepare to change direction. (Note: don't push the outside step too far out on the shuffle, or you will have difficulty getting back to the ladder.)

The Cross-Step, on the other hand, lends itself nicely to the biggest bound you can safely make as you leave the ladder and and leap out to the side. *(see illustration, previous page.)* Start this exercise standing well out to the left side of the ladder with your right foot lifted off the ground. Your first step will be to place the (formerly) lifted right foot down near the ladder. Then you cross your left foot in the square, and bound off that foot as far as you can to land on the right foot, then repeat in the other direction. Change your word cue to this: "Step-cross-bound!" Try to land the bound fully balanced before you worry about trying to increase the speed of your cutback to the ladder.

LATERAL SPEED & AGILITY - BALANCE/ BODY AWARENESS

90 Degree Jumps — *see illustration*
Off two feet, jump and turn 90 degrees and then jump and return to the start. Add 90 degrees to each jump until it becomes a complete 360 jump.

180 Degree Jumps — *see illustration*
Off two feet jump, and turn 180 degrees. Repeat to the opposite direction.

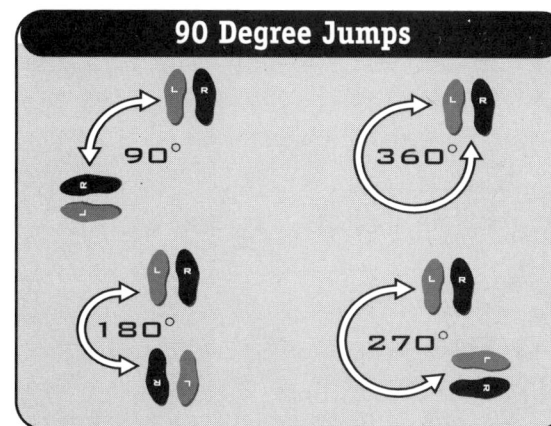

90 Degree Jumps

180 Degree Jumps

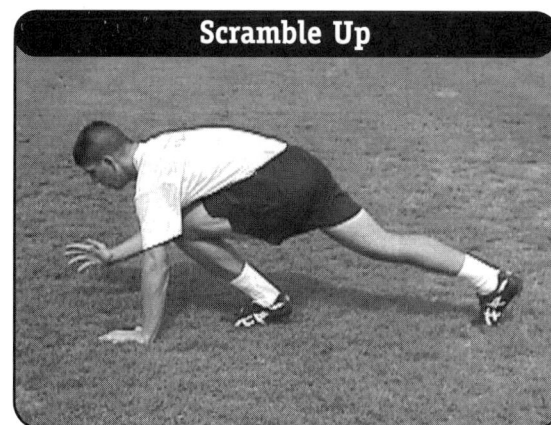

Scramble Up

Scramble Up — *see photo, previous page.*

a) Onto two feet – end in athletic position

b) Onto one leg

Lying face down with the hands placed at the side of the chest, scramble up as fast as possible onto one leg and balance for two counts.

c) React

Lying face down with the hands placed at the side of the chest, scramble up as fast as possible onto two feet, react to another player or the ball.

Medicine Ball Stepping Stones

— see photos

Use leather medicine balls that will compress slightly when stepped on. Place the ball in a scattered pattern about two to three feet apart. Step from one ball to the other either alternating feet or stepping onto the same ball with one foot and then the other. It is also good to balance and hold for three to five seconds on each ball.

Dot Drill — *see illustration*

Starting Position: Left foot on A and right foot on B.

Step One: Step to 1 with right foot and D with left foot.

Step Two: Step to C with right foot and step back to 1 with left foot.

Step Three: Step to B with right foot and back to A with left foot.

Medicine Ball Stepping Stones

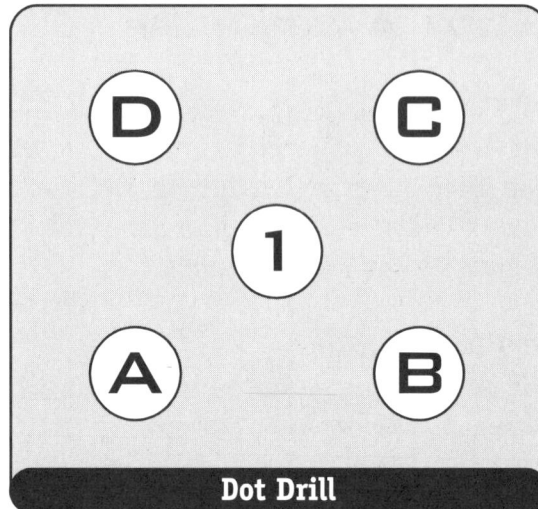
Dot Drill

Repeat five times with the same pattern, then switch to right foot lead. There are numerous variations of this drill. Once mastery is achieved, add a ball to make it more challenging.

LATERAL SPEED & AGILITY - OBSTACLE AVOIDANCE

Rubber Band Step Over (Inside foot)

Anchor a piece of rubber tubing between two points eight to ten feet apart, six to eight inches in height. Step over to the opposite side and return leading with the inside foot while moving as quickly as

Rubber Band Step Over

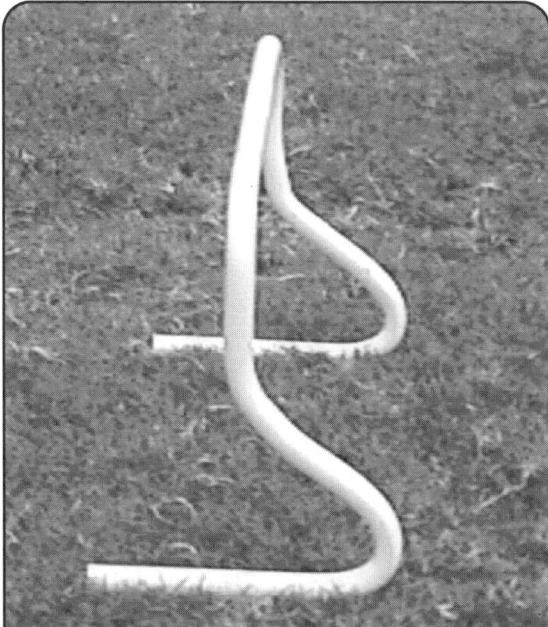
Little Hurdles (Twelve Inch)

One Band

Uphill/Downhill
Execute any of the previously mentioned drills that would be appropriate. Use the uphill for resistance and the downhill for assistance.

Cobra
Execute the drill for a number of touches or a set time. Remember to keep the time frame short because the objective is speed.
  a) One Band — *see photo*
  b) Two Bands — *see photo*

possible down the tubing. Pay particular attention to stepping, not jumping the tubing. Remember time in the air is time wasted. *see photo*

Little Hurdles (Twelve Inch)
— *see photo*
Have the player run through the hurdles with the emphasis on getting the feet down quickly, not floating in the air.
  a) Run forward
  b) Run sideways

Two Bands

SPEED-COACHING POINTS & CUES

Speed is a motor task; therefore, you can learn to run faster through correct mechanics and improved situational awareness.

Speed development must be done while rested. To learn correct technique, speed development work should occur at the start of the workout following an easy work day or a rest day.

Demand correct mechanics and relate the mechanics to the specific movements of soccer both with and without the ball. Perfect practice makes permanent.

Optimum speed is the goal: speed you can use and control in the game of soccer.

Never lose sight of speed as the "moment of truth." When you least expect it and are most fatigued speed will win the game.

Speed work demands the highest level of motivation and concentration.

Initiate movement with a fall from the center, not with the head and shoulders. This will ensure balance with each step, and will also ensure the ability to change direction or shift weight as demanded by the ball or the opponent.

Quick hands when starting: The hands are the trigger and the arms are the gun. A world class sprinter in the starting blocks moves the hands first in order to put pressure back against the blocks. Even though a soccer player does not use starting blocks this principle can be applied to an upright posture. Think quick hands to initiate movement!

Big arms when accelerating: Drive the arms down and back – Hammer back! This will help you to apply more force against the ground with each step in order to overcome inertia.

Create a positive shin angle both straight ahead and in lateral speed & agility. This will put you in a position to use the largest and strongest muscles of the legs to push and extend.

Keep the hips over the feet at all times for balance and the ability to move laterally.

Starting is extending: Use triple extension and pushing from the ankle/knee/hip.

First step quickness is moving the center of gravity in the intended direction.

Movement of the center of gravity up or down is wasted movement.

Length of First Step(s): Get the foot down. You can only apply force with the foot on the ground. Getting the foot down quickly will create a positive shin angle. Too long a first step will create a negative shin angle which forces a pulling action rather than a pushing action; this is very inefficient.

Stopping is bending ankle/knee/hip in order to reduce force over as many joints as possible. Learning to stop efficiently will improve your soccer skills as well as prevent injury.

Game Speed effort is necessary to improve speed. Learn at a speed you can control, then once the drill or the action is mastered practice at game speed. Anything less than game speed will not help to improve your speed once technique has been mastered.

Reaction can be improved by working on the primary stimulus which is visual (either the ball or another player).

Adequate strength as expressed by the ability to control one's own bodyweight and sound basic technique is prerequisite for speed development.

Vary speed training methods and intensity to avoid building a speed barrier.

SPEED WORKOUT ORGANIZATION

What should I do?
Some aspect of speed training should be part of daily training throughout the train-ing year. Either acceleration or lateral speed and agility work can be done as many as four days a week if it is sequenced properly.

How should I do it?
What equipment do I need?
It is best if you get a partner to work with you. The equipment needs are minimal. (See equipment list in the appendix at the end of the book.)

When should I do my speed development work?
Try to do it early in practice or workout while you are in a non-fatigued state. Speed endurance work can be done during practice or after practice when the player is tired. Speed Endurance should only be done after the player has mastered good mechanics so that fatigue will not compromise the quality of the movement. Remember, the principle is speed before speed endurance.

What should I consider in determining the workload?
- *Time of the training year.* Earlier in the year there should be greater volume. Volume should be reduced as the year progresses.
- *Total number of yards or meters.* This should be based on game analysis. The number of top speed efforts and the pattern of running should reflect the player's position and style of play.
- *The number of exercises or drills.* Five to eight drills executed properly at game speed is preferable to more drills.
- *The work to rest ratio.* A ratio of one: three or more is preferable for optimum speed results.
- *What to do during recovery.* Be active. Work on balance or reaction, do not waste the time. Soccer is a game that demands total concentration, so practice this by being fully engaged even during the recovery time.
- *Fast people must run fast!* If you have players who are gifted with speed make sure to keep training speed. Law of reversibility—use it or lose it!

How should I determine the distribution of work?
- *How often in a microcycle?* To develop speed it is best to do a little bit more often. Four workouts devoted to some component of speed per week will yield best results.
- *What is the cumulative training effect?* If the sequence is proper and enough time is allowed for recovery, then the results will be very positive.

BALANCING THE TRAINING COMPONENTS

The training components must be sequenced so as to not overload the system. The components must be related to what will be done during practice and after practice. The following is a sequence that works well in the off-season when there are no games scheduled.

DAY ONE	DAY TWO	DAY THREE	DAY FOUR	DAY FIVE
SpAc	LSA		SpAc	LSA
Plyo's			Plyo's	
Core Work	Core Work	Core Work	Core Work	Core Work

SPEED DEVELOPMENT WORKOUT ORGANIZATION

Warm-up:
Dovetail this to the actual workout. *(See warm-up section)*

Pre-Practice:
Use this to set the tempo and create a readiness for the work to follow.

During Practice:
If possible include some highly specific speed work distributed throughout practice.

Post-Practice:
Not an optimum time. Use only as a last resort.

When you are designing a program, choose five to eight drills daily. Have a specific objective for each of the drills relative to the players strengths and weaknesses. The total time devoted to speed development drills should be about fifteen to twenty minutes total per day. Remember that the drills do not have to be done all at once, they can be distributed throughout practice to complement soccer skills. Be sure to allow enough rest between drills so that quality is maintained. In the beginning stages, technique is more important that speed. Learn to execute the action correctly then add speed.

Design soccer specific drills that are derivatives of the generic speed development drills. This will ensure that the improved speed will transfer to the game.

SPEED WORKOUT GROUPING

By Position:
This is the easiest and most practical approach.

By Strengths/Weaknesses:
This is most effective to group by speed based on test performance, but not always practical.

Arbitrary Groups:
This is probably the least effective.

EXERCISE AND TRAINING METHODS SELECTION CONSIDERATIONS

- Time frame available. Be realistic. Remember they are preparing for soccer, not a track meet.
- Difficulty in teaching. Do not try to make it too complex. Pick drills that are appropriate for the level of player.
- Equipment needs. What equipment do you need? Try not to have the workouts based on too much equipment as that can be a limiting factor in getting the workout done.

MEETING INDIVIDUAL NEEDS IN A GROUP CONTEXT

This is the key to the programs effectiveness, since soccer is a team sport. It is best to group by ability wherever possible.

Try to make the groups as small and as specific as possible.

FORMATIONS & LINES

This can have a huge impact on the effectiveness of the workout. Start by determining the number of athletes. Then determine the number of lines. Then divide the number of lines into the number of athletes to determine the number in each line. No more than six lines. Three or four lines is preferable. Four to six in a line will give the proper amount of rest. For teaching, use a staggered formation with a quarter turn to the right to allow all the athletes to view the instruction.

EVALUATIVE CRITERIA FOR DRILLS OR EXERCISES

When selecting the drills and exercises always ask the following questions:
- Is it functional?
- How does it relate to the actual movement being trained for?
- Does the athlete relate it?
- Is it adaptable?

STRAIGHT AHEAD SPEED (SAS) EXERCISE MENU

SAS — Starting Acceleration

Soccer Start
Stagger Start
Walking Start
Running Start
Downhill Start
Dancing Start
  a) W/O Reaction
  b) With Reaction
Side Step & Go
Crossover Step & Go
Jump & Go
Scramble Out
Seat Roll & Go
Forward Roll & Go
Drop Step & Go
180 Jump & Go
Plant & Drive Off
Push & Go
Shoulder Bump & Go
Slide Tackle Start
Low Box Starts
Seated Start
Stick Drill

SAS — Decision Making Speed

Decision Making Start
  a) In Place
  b) Forward
Low Five
Give & Go
Give-Go-Get
Give-Go-Get & Turn
Numbered Cones

SAS — Speed in Cooperation

Two Player Serpentine
Two Player Weave
Three Player Weave
Single File Weave
Follow the Leader

SAS — Resistance

Two Hops & Sprint
Four Bounds into Sprint
Harness
Sled or Tire Pull
Contrast (Harness or Sled)
Hill Sprints
Parachute
  a) Forward
  b) Backward
  c) Weave
Sand Sprints
Contrast – Sand to grass
Uphill to Level
Downhill to Level

SAS — Assistance

Towing
  a) Short Pull
  b) Long Pull
Downhill
Flying Sprint

LATERAL SPEED AND AGILITY (LSA) EXERCISE MENU

LSA — Reaction/Recognition

Ball Drop
a) One Ball
b) Two Ball
Z Ball
Ball Roll
Recognition Hoops
Reaction Belt
Reaction Runs
a) Same direction
b) Opposite direction
Wave Drill

LSA — Footwork

Jump Rope
- Double Leg Jumps
- Stride Jumps
- Crossover Jumps
- Single Leg Hops

Low Box Quickstep
Line Step Over
Cone Step Over
Hoops Double-In
Little Hurdles (Six Inch)
a) Even Rhythm
b) Broken Rhythm
Speed/Agility Ladder Basic Series
- Forward One In
- Forward Two In
- Lateral Two-In
- Two In Ali Shuffle
- One In Ali Shuffle

LSA — Change of Direction

Quarter Eagle
a) Run Out
b) Run Out & Return
Scramble Out
a) Run Out
b) Run Out & Return
Z Band
a) Plant & Cut
b) Plant & Cut & Return
Slalom Flags
a) Weave
b) Slalom
c) Plant & Cut
d) Plant & Shuffle
5-10-5 Change Series
a) Shuffle
b) Carioca
c) Back & Forward
d) Side to Side
Speed/Agility Ladder Change of Direction
Footwork Drills
- Forward Slalom Jumps
- Backward Slalom Jumps
- Three Count Shuffle – Forward
- Three Count Shuffle – Backward
- Forward Cross-Steps
- Backward Cross-Steps
- Forward Shuffle-Bounds
- Backward Shuffle-Bounds
- Forward Cross-Step-Bounds
- Backward Cross-Step-Bounds

LSA – Balance/Body Awareness

90 Degree Jumps
180 Degree Jumps
Scramble Up
a) Onto One Leg
b) React
Medicine Ball Stepping Stone
Dot Drill

LSA — Obstacle Avoidance

Band Step Over (Inside foot)
Little Hurdles
a) Forward
b) Lateral
Uphill/Downhill
Cobra
a) One Band
b) Two Bands

WORKOUT EXPLANATION

Teach - Means that the drill must be thoroughly taught and mastered by the player before it can be used in a training session. Remember a drill done incorrectly will result in an incorrect motor pattern which could do more harm than good.

Train – Means that the drill is regularly incorporated into the training program.

EMPHASIS EXPLANATION

—

Not a major emphasis during that particular training period. The drill or exercise will be incorporated into the training plan no more than once a week.

0

Do only as needed to maintain that particular quality. Maximum of two times per week.

+

A major emphasis. At least two times and sometimes three times every seven days.

DRILL CATEGORY: SAS STARTING ACCELERATION

Name of Drill	Page #	Youth	Developing	Elite	Off Season	Pre Season	In Season
Soccer Start	20	Teach/Trn	Train	Train	+	+	0
Stagger Start	24	Teach/Trn	Train	Train	+	+	0
Walking Start	24	Teach/Trn	Train	Train	+	0	
Running Start	24	Teach/Trn	Train	Train	0	+	+
Downhill Start	24		Teach/Trn	Train		+	0
Dancing Start	24	Teach/Trn	Train	Train	+	+	+
Side step & Go	24	Teach/Trn	Train	Train	-	0	0
Crossover Step & Go	25	Teach/Trn	Train	Train	-	0	0
Jump & Go	25	Teach/Trn	Train	Train	+	+	0
Scramble Out	25	Teach/Trn	Train	Train	+	+	0
Seat Roll & Go	25	Teach/Trn	Train	Train	+	0	-
Forward roll & Go	26	Teach/Trn	Train	Train	+	0	-
Drop Step & Go	26		Teach/Trn	Train	+	+	0
180 Jump & Go	26	Teach/Trn	Train	Train	+	+	0
Plant & Drive Off	26	Teach	Train	Train	+	+	0
Push & Go	26		Teach/Trn	Train	-	+	+
Shoulder Bump & Go	26	Teach/Trn	Train	Train	-	+	+
Slide Tackle Start	27		Teach/Trn	Train	-	+	0
Low Box Starts	27	Teach/Trn	Train	Train	0	+	
Seated Start	28	Teach/Trn	Train	Train		+	
Stick Drill	29		Teach/Trn	Train		+	

- = Minor Emphasis   o = Maintain   + = Major Emphasis

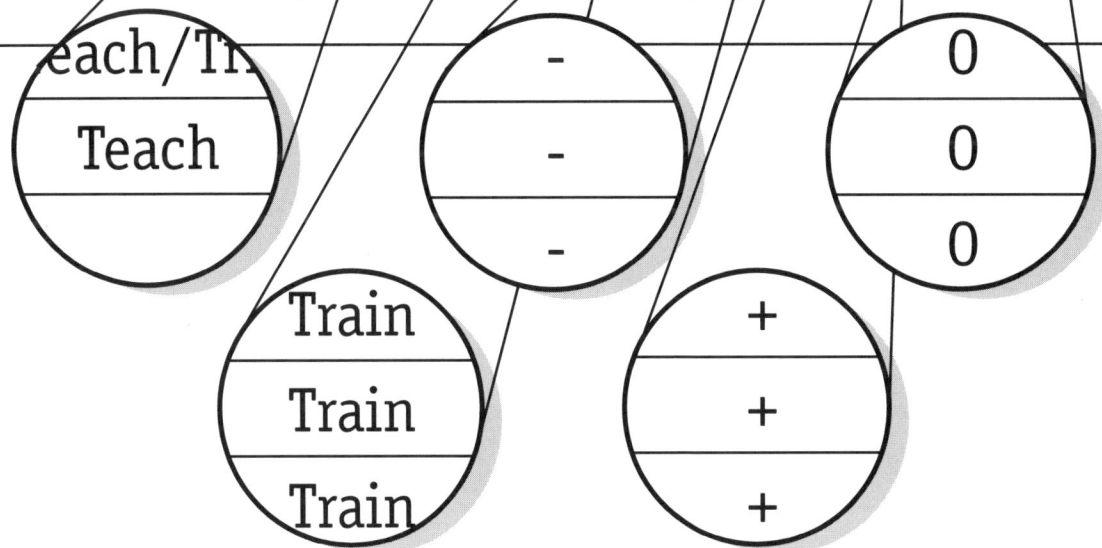

Teach/Trn

Teach

Train
Train
Train

-
-
-

+
+
+

0
0
0

53

Drill Category: SAS Starting Acceleration

Name of Drill	Page #	Youth	Developing	Elite	Off Season	Pre Season	In Season
Soccer Start	20	Teach/Trn	Train	Train	+	+	0
Stagger Start	24	Teach/Trn	Train	Train	+	+	0
Walking Start	24	Teach/Trn	Train	Train	+	0	
Running Start	24	Teach/Trn	Train	Train	0	+	+
Downhill Start	24		Teach/Trn	Train		+	0
Dancing Start	24	Teach/Trn	Train	Train	+	+	+
Side Step & Go	24	Teach/Trn	Train	Train	-	0	0
Crossover Step & Go	25	Teach/Trn	Train	Train	-	0	0
Jump & Go	25	Teach/Trn	Train	Train	+	+	0
Scramble Out	25	Teach/Trn	Train	Train	+	+	0
Seat Roll & Go	25	Teach/Trn	Train	Train	+	0	-
Forward Roll & Go	26	Teach/Trn	Train	Train	+	0	-
Drop Step & Go	26		Teach/Trn	Train	+	+	0
180 Jump & Go	26	Teach/Trn	Train	Train	+	+	0
Plant & Drive Off	26	Teach	Train	Train	+	+	0
Push & Go	26		Teach/Trn	Train	-	+	+
Shoulder Bump & Go	26	Teach/Trn	Train	Train	-	+	+
Slide Tackle Start	27		Teach/Trn	Train	-	+	0
Low Box Starts	27	Teach/Trn	Train	Train	0	+	
Seated Start	28	Teach/Trn	Train	Train		+	
Stick Drill	29		Teach/Trn	Train		+	

- = Minor Emphasis   o = Maintain   + = Major Emphasis

Drill Category: SAS Decision Making Speed

Name of Drill	Page #	Youth	Developing	Elite	Off Season	Pre Season	In Season
Decision Making Start	28	Teach/Trn	Train	Train		+	0
Low Five	28	Teach/Trn	Train	Train	+	0	
Give & Go	28	Teach/Trn	Train	Train	-	+	+
Give-Go-Get	28	Teach/Trn	Train	Train	-	+	+
Give-Go-Get & Turn	29		Teach/Trn	Train	-	+	+
Numbered Cones	29	Teach/Trn	Train	Train	-	+	+

- = Minor Emphasis   o = Maintain   + = Major Emphasis

Drill Category: SAS Speed in Cooperation

Name of Drill	Page #	Youth	Developing	Elite	Off Season	Pre Season	In Season
Two Player Serpentine	29	Teach/Trn	Train	Train	-	+	0
Two Player Weave	29	Teach/Trn	Train	Train	-	+	0
Three Player Weave	30	Teach/Trn	Train	Train	-	+	0
Single File Weave	30	Teach/Trn	Train	Train	-	+	0
Follow The Leader	30	Teach/Trn	Train	Train	-	+	0

- = Minor Emphasis   o = Maintain   + = Major Emphasis

Drill Category: SAS Resistance

Name of Drill	Page #	Youth	Developing	Elite	Off Season	Pre Season	In Season
Two Hops & Sprint	31	Teach/Trn	Train	Train		+	0
Four Bounds into Sprint	31		Teach/Trn	Train		+	0
Harness	31		Teach/Trn	Train	+	+	0
Sled or Tire Pull	31	Teach/Trn	Train	Train	+	+	0
Contrast	31	Teach/Trn	Train	Train		+	+
Parachute – Forward	32	Teach/Trn	Train	Train		+	0
Parachute – Backward	32	Teach/Trn	Train	Train		+	0
Parachute – Weave	32	Teach/Trn	Train	Train		+	0
Sand Sprints	32	Teach/Trn	Train	Train	+		

- = Minor Emphasis   o = Maintain   + = Major Emphasis

Drill Category: SAS Absolute Speed

Name of Drill	Page #	Youth	Developing	Elite	Off Season	Pre Season	In Season
Towing – Short Pull	33		Teach/Trn	Train	0	+	+
Towing – Long Pull	33		Teach/Trn	Train		+	0
Downhill	33	Teach/Trn	Train	Train		+	
Flying Sprint	33	Teach/Trn	Train	Train		+	0

- = Minor Emphasis   o = Maintain   + = Major Emphasis

DRILL CATEGORY: LSA REACTION/RECOGNITION

Name of Drill	Page #	Youth	Developing	Elite	Off Season	Pre Season	In Season
Ball Drop- One Ball	36	Teach/Trn	Train	Train	+	+	0
Ball Drop – Two Balls	36	Teach/Trn	Train	Train	+	+	0
Z Ball	36	Teach/Trn	Train	Train	+	+	0
Ball Roll	36	Teach/Trn	Train	Train	+	+	0
Recognition Hoops	36	Teach/Trn	Train	Train	0	+	
Reaction Belt	36	Teach/Trn	Train	Train	0	+	
Reaction Run – Same Direction	36	Teach/Trn	Train	Train	+	+	0
Reaction Run – Opposite Direction	36	Teach/Trn	Train	Train	+	+	0
Wave Drill	36	Teach/Trn	Train	Train		+	+

- = Minor Emphasis   o = Maintain   + = Major Emphasis

DRILL CATEGORY: LSA FOOTWORK

Name of Drill	Page #	Youth	Developing	Elite	Off Season	Pre Season	In Season
Jump Rope Routine	37	Teach/Trn	Train	Train	+	+	+
Low Box Quickstep	37	Teach/Trn	Train	Train	+	+	0
Line Step Over	38	Teach/Trn	Train	Train	+	+	+
Cone Step Over	38		Teach/Trn	Train			
Hoops Double In	38	Teach/Trn	Train	Train	+	+	+
Little Hurdles – Even	40	Teach/Trn	Train	Train	+	+	+
Little Hurdles – Broken	40	Teach/Trn	Train	Train	+	+	+
SL Forward One In	38	Teach/Trn	Train	Train	+	+	+
SL Forward Two In	38	Teach/Trn	Train	Train	+	+	+
SL Lateral Two In	38	Teach/Trn	Train	Train	+	+	+
SL Lateral Cross-step	38		Teach/Trn	Train	+	+	+
SL Two in Ali Shuffle	38	Teach/Trn	Train	Train	+	+	0
SL One in Ali Shuffle	40	Teach/Trn	Train	Train	+	+	0

- = Minor Emphasis   o = Maintain   + = Major Emphasis   SL = Speed Ladder

DRILL CATEGORY: LSA CHANGE OF DIRECTION

Name of Drill	Page #	Youth	Developing	Elite	Off Season	Pre Season	In Season
Quarter Eagle – Run Out	40	Teach	Train	Train	+	+	0
Quarter Eagle – Run Out & Return	40	Teach	Train	Train	+	+	0
Scramble Out – Run Out & Return	40	Teach/Trn	Train	Train	+	0	
Z Band – Plant & Cut	40	Teach/Trn	Train	Train	+	+	0
Z Band – Plant & Cut & Return	40	Teach/Trn	Train	Train	+	+	0
Flags - Weave	41	Teach/Trn	Train	Train	+	+	+
Flags – Slalom	41	Teach/Trn	Train	Train	+	+	+
Flags – Plant & Cut	41	Teach/Trn	Train	Train	+	+	+
Flags – Plant & Shuffle	41	Teach/Trn	Train	Train	+	+	+
5-10-5 - Series	42	Teach/Trn	Train	Train	+	0	
SL Forward Slalom Jump	43	Teach/Trn	Train	Train	+	+	0
SL Backward Slalom Jump	43	Teach/Trn	Train	Train	+	+	0
SL 3 Count Shuffle - Forward	42	Teach/Trn	Train	Train	+	+	+
SL 3 Count Shuffle - Backward	42	Teach/Trn	Train	Train	+	+	+
SL Forward Cross Step	43		Teach/Trn	Train	+	+	+
SL Backward Cross Step	44		Teach/Trn	Train	+	+	+
SL Forward Shuffle Bound	44		Teach/Trn	Train	+	+	+
SL Backward Shuffle Bound	44		Teach/Trn	Train	+	+	+
SL Forward Cross Step - Bound	43	Teach/Trn	Train	+	+	+	
SL Backward Cross Step - Bound	44		Teach/Trn	Train	+	+	+

- = Minor Emphasis   o = Maintain   + = Major Emphasis

Drill Category: LSA Balance/Body Awareness

Name of Drill	Page #	Youth	Developing	Elite	Off Season	Pre Season	In Season
90 Degree Jumps	45	Teach/Trn	Train	Train	+	+	0
180 Degree Jumps	45	Teach/Trn	Train	Train	+	+	0
Scramble Up onto One Leg	45	Teach/Trn	Train	Train	+	0	
Scramble Up & React	46	Teach/Trn	Train	Train	+	0	
Med Ball Stepping Stone	46	Teach/Trn	Train	Train	+	+	0
Dot Drill	46		Teach/Trn	Train	+	+	0

- = Minor Emphasis   o = Maintain   + = Major Emphasis

Drill Category: LSA Obstacle Avoidance

Name of Drill	Page #	Youth	Developing	Elite	Off Season	Pre Season	In Season
Band Stepover	46	Teach/Trn	Train	Train	+	+	
Little Hurdles – Forward	47	Teach/Trn	Train	Train	+	+	-
Little Hurdles - Lateral	47	Teach/Trn	Train	Train	+	+	+

- = Minor Emphasis   o = Maintain   + = Major Emphasis

Drill Category: LSA Drill Resistance

Name of Drill	Page #	Youth	Developing	Elite	Off Season	Pre Season	In Season
Uphill/Downhill	47		Teach/Trn	Train	+		
Cobra – One Band	47		Teach/Trn	Train	+	+	0
Cobra – Two bands	47		Teach/Trn	Train	+	+	0

- = Minor Emphasis   o = Maintain   + = Major Emphasis

Training Phase: Off-season — Objective: teach and master the execution the drills

MONDAY (SAS Emphasis)
• **Warm-up #1**
• **Soccer Start** x 3 @ 15 yards
• **Stagger Start** x 3 Right & 3 Left @ 10 yards
• **Walking Start** x 3 Right & 3 Left @ 10 yards
• **Sidestep & Go** x 3 Right & 3 Left @ 10 yards
• **Crossover Step** & Go x 3 Right & 3 Left @ 10 yards
• **Harness** x 6 @ 20 yards

TUESDAY (LSA Emphasis)
• **Warm-up #2**
• **Single Leg Squat Balance** (Hold each position ten counts)
• **Balance Shift** (Hold each position six to ten counts)
• **Quarter Eagle** x 3 Right & 3 Left
• **Z Band** - Plant & Cut x 3
• **Flag Series** x 2 of each drill
• **Speed/Agility Ladder Routine** (Choose four drills, 3 repetitions of each)

WEDNESDAY
• **Warm-up #1**
• **Ball Drop** – One Ball x 6
• **Ball Roll** x 6
• **Speed Ladder** (Choose four drills 3 repetitions of each)
• **Soccer Skill** – Small sided games incorporating SAS & LSA concepts.

THURSDAY (SAS Emphasis)
• **Warm-up #1**
• **Soccer Start** x 3 @ 15 yards
• **Stagger Start** x 3 Right & 3 Left @ 20 yards
• **Jump & Go** x 4 @ 10 yards
• **Scramble Out** x 4 @ 10 yards
• **Seat Roll & Go** x 2 Right & 2 Left @ 10 yards
• **Harness** x 6 @ 20 yards

FRIDAY (LSA emphasis)
• **Warm-up #2**
• **Single Leg Squat Balance** (Hold each position ten counts)
• **Balance Shift** (Hold each position six to ten counts)
• **Quarter Eagle** x 3 Right & 3 Left
• **Z Band** - Plant & Cut x 3
• **Flag Series** x 2 of each drill
• **Speed/Agility Ladder Routine** (Choose four drills 3 repetitions of each)
• **Little Hurdles** – Even x 8 Hurdles x 4
• **One Eighty Jumps** x 4 (2 Left and 2 Right)

SATURDAY
• **Warm-up #2**
• **Ball Drop** – One Ball x 6
• **Ball Roll** x 6
• **Speed Ladder** (Choose four drills 3 repetitions of each)
• **Soccer Skill** – Small sided games incorporating SAS & LSA concepts.

Training Phase: Pre-season — Objective: Incorporate SAS and LSA components into more soccer specific movements

MONDAY (SAS Emphasis)
• **Warm-up #1**
• **Soccer Start** x 3 @ 15 yards
• **Stagger Start** x 3 Right & 3 Left @ 10 yards
• **Walking Start** x 3 Right & 3 Left @ 10 yards
• **Running Start** 3 Right & 3 Left @ 15 yards
• **Dancing Start** 2 Right & 2 Left @ 20 yards
• **Two Hops & Sprint** 2 Right & 2 Left @ 10 yards

TUESDAY (LSA Emphasis)
• **Warm-up #2**
• **Single Leg Squat Balance** (Hold each position ten counts)
• **Balance Shift** (Hold each position six to ten counts)
• **Quarter Eagle** x 3 Right & 3 Left
• **Z Band** - Plant & Cut x 3
• **Flag Series** x 2 of each drill
• **Speed/Agility Ladder Routine** (Choose four drills, 3 repetitions of each)
• **Ninety Degree Jumps** x 3 Right & 3 Left

WEDNESDAY
• **Warm-up #1**
• **Shoulder Bump & Go** 3 @ 10 yards
• **Give & Go** x 3 @ 20 yards
• **Give/Go/Get** x 3 @ 20 yards
• **Give/Go & Turn** x 3 @ 20 yards
• **Ball Drop** – Two Ball x 6
• **Reaction Run** x 4 @ 10 yards
• **Speed Ladder** (Choose four drills, 3 repetitions of each)
• **Soccer Skill** – Small sided games incorporating SAS & LSA concepts.

THURSDAY (SAS Emphasis)
• **Warm-up #1**
• **Soccer Start** x 3 @ 15 yards
• **Stagger Start** x 3 Right & 3 Left @ 20 yards
• **Running Start** - Hit a mark x 3 Right & 3 Left @ 10 yards
• **Running Start** - Hit a mark x 3 Right & 3 Left @ 10 yards
• **Dancing Start** x 3 @ 15 yards
• **Sled or Tire** Pull x 6 @ 25 yards

FRIDAY (LSA emphasis)
• **Warm-up #2**
• **Single Leg Squat Balance** (Hold each position ten counts)
• **Balance Shift** (Hold each position Six to Ten counts)
• **Quarter Eagle** x 3 right & 3 left
• **Flag Series** x 2 of each drill
• **Speed/Agility Ladder Routine** (Chose four drills, 3 repetitions of each)
• **Little Hurdles** – Even 4 x 6-8 hurdles
• **One Eighty Jumps** x 3 right and 3 left

SATURDAY
• **Warm-up #2**
• **Two Player Weave** x 2 @ 20 yards
• **Follow the Leader** x 2 @ 20 yards
• **Ball Drop** – Two Balls x 4
• **Reaction Run** x 2 @ 10 yards
• **Scrimmage** 11 vs. 11

Training Phase: In-season — Objective: Reduce the volume of work, emphasize quality of effort.

MONDAY (SAS Emphasis)
• **Warm-up #1**
• **Stagger Start** x 3 Right & 3 Left @ 10 yards
• **Balance Start** x 3 Right & 3 Left @ 10 yards
• **Running Start** 3 Right & 3 Left @ 10 yards
• **Dancing Start** 2 Right & 2 Left @ 10 yards
• **Jump & Go** 2 Right & 2 Left @ 10 yards
• **Ninety Degree Jumps** x 3 Right & 3 Left

TUESDAY (LSA Emphasis)
• **Single Leg Squat Balance** (Hold each position ten counts)
• **Balance Shift** (Hold each position six to ten counts)
• **Flag Series** x 2 of each drill
• **Speed/Agility Ladder Routine** (Choose four drills, 3 repetitions of each)
• **Little Hurdles** – Even 4 x 6 hurdles

WEDNESDAY
• **Numbered Cones** x 4
• **Three Player Weave** x 4 @ 20 yards
• **Reaction Run** x 4 @ 20 yards
• **Ball drop** – Two Balls x 4

THURSDAY (SAS Emphasis)
• **Warm-up #1**
• **Stagger Start** x 3 Right & 3 Left @ 10 yards
• **Balance Start** x 3 Right & 3 Left @ 10 yards
• **Running Start** 3 Right & 3 Left @ 10 yards
• **Dancing Start** 2 Right & 2 Left @ 10 yards
• **Jump & Go** 2 Right & 2 Left @ 10 yards
• **One Eighty Jumps** x 3 Right & 3 Left

FRIDAY (LSA emphasis)
• **Single Leg Squat Balance** (Hold each position ten counts)
• **Balance Shift** (Hold each position six to ten counts)
• **Speed/Agility Ladder Routine** (Choose four drills, 2 repetitions of each)

SATURDAY
Game

DEVELOPING

Training Phase: Off-season   **Objective: Learn the routine of training and master execution of drills. Highest volume of work.**

MONDAY (SAS Emphasis)
- **Warm-up #1**
- **Soccer Start** x 4 @ 10 yards
- **Stagger Start** x 4 Right & 4 Left @ 10 yards
- **Balance Start** x 4 Right & 4 Left @ 10 yards
- **Walking Start** x 3 Right & 3 Left @ 20 yards
- **Sidestep & Go** x 3 Right & 3 Left @ 10 yards
- **Crossover Step & Go** x 3 Right & 3 Left @ 10 yards
- **Harness or Sled** x 6-8 @ 20 yards

TUESDAY (LSA Emphasis)
- **Warm-up #2**
- **Single Leg Squat Balance** (Hold each position ten counts)
- **Balance Shift** (Hold each position six to ten counts)
- **Quarter Eagle** x 3 Right & 3 Left with a 10 yard sprint out
- **Z Band** 2 of each drill a) Plant & Cut b) Plant & Cut & Return c) Stepover (Inside foot)
- **Flag Series** 3 of each drill
- **Speed/Agility Ladder Routine** (Choose five drills, 3 repetitions of each)

WEDNESDAY
- **Warm-up #1**
- **Decision Making Start** x 6 @ 10 yards
- **Ball Drop** – One Ball x 6
- **Ball Roll** x 6
- **Speed Ladder** (Choose six drills, 3 repetitions of each)
- **Give & Go** x 3 @ 30 yards
- **Give & Go & Get** x 3 @ 30 yards
- **Soccer Skill** – Small sided games incorporating SAS & LSA concepts.

THURSDAY (SAS Emphasis)
- **Warm-up #1**
- **Soccer Start** x 3 @ 15 yards
- **Stagger Start** x 3 Right & 3 Left @ 20 yards
- **Balance Start** x 3 Right & 3 Left @ 10 yards
- **Jump & Go** x 4 @ 10 yards
- **Scramble Out** x 4 @ 10 yards
- **Seat Roll & Go** x 2 Right & 2 Left @ 10 yards
- **Harness or Sled** x 6-8 @ 20 yards

FRIDAY (LSA emphasis)
- **Warm-up #2**
- **Single Leg Squat Balance** (Hold each position ten counts)
- **Balance Shift** (Hold each position six to ten counts)
- **Quarter Eagle** x 3 Right & 3 Left with 10 yard sprint out & return
- **Z Band** x 2 of each drill a) Plant & Cut b) Plant & Cut & Return c) Stepover (Inside foot)
- **Flag Series** x 3 of each drill
- **Speed/Agility Ladder Routine** (Choose 4 drills, 2 repetitions of each)
- **Little Hurdles** – Even 6 x 6 hurdles
- **One Eighty Jumps** x 3 Right & 3 Left

SATURDAY
- **Warm-up #2**
- **Decision Making Start** x 4 @ 10 yards
- **Ball Drop** – One Ball x 6
- **Ball Roll** x 6
- **Speed Ladder** (Choose six drills, 2 repetitions of each)
- **Give & Go** x 3 @ 30 yards
- **Give & Go & Get** x 3 @ 30 yards
- **Soccer Skill** – Small sided games incorporating SAS & LSA concepts.

Training Phase: Pre-season   **Objective: Volume should remain high, but intensity should also rise. Transition to more soccer specific activities.**

MONDAY (SAS Emphasis)
- **Warm-up #1**
- **Soccer Start** x 3 @ 15 yards
- **Stagger Start** x 3 Right & 3 Left @ 20 yards
- **Balance Start** x 3 Right & 3 Left @ 20 yards
- **Running Start** 3 Right & 3 Left @ 15 yards
- **Dancing Start** 2 Right & 2 Left @ 20 yards
- **Two Hops & Sprint** 2 Right & 2 Left @ 20 yards
- **Four Bounds into Sprint** x 4

TUESDAY (LSA Emphasis)
- **Warm-up #2**
- **Single Leg Squat Balance** (Hold each position ten counts)
- **Balance Shift** (Hold each position Six to Ten counts)
- **Quarter Eagle** x 3 Right & 3 Left with 10 yard sprint out
- **Z Band** x 2 of each drill a) Plant & Cut b) Plant & Cut & Return c) Stepover (Inside foot)
- **Hoops Double** In 6 x 6 hoops
- **Flag Series** 2 of each drill
- **Speed/Agility Ladder Routine** (Choose 6 drills, 3 repetitions of each)
- **Ninety Degree Jumps** x 3 Right & 3 Left

WEDNESDAY
- **Warm-up #1**
- **Shoulder Bump & Go** 3 @ 15 yards
- **Give & Go** x 2 @ 30 yards
- **Give/Go/Get** x 2 @ 30 yards
- **Give/Go & Turn** x 2 @ 30 yards
- **Ball Drop** – Two Ball x 6
- **Reaction Run** x 4 @ 10 yards
- **Speed/Agility Ladder Routine** (Choose four drills, 2 repetitions of each)
- **Soccer Skill** – Small sided games incorporating SAS & LSA concepts.

THURSDAY (SAS Emphasis)
- **Warm-up #1**
- **Soccer Start** x 3 @ 15 yards
- **Stagger Start** x 3 Right & 3 Left @ 20 yards
- **Balance Start** x 3 Right & 3 Left @ 10 yards
- **Running Start** 3 Right & 3 Left @ 15 yards
- **Dancing Start** x 3 Right & 3 Left @ 15 yards
- **Sled or Tire Pull** x 4-6 @ 20 yards

FRIDAY (LSA emphasis)
- **Warm-up #2**
- **Single Leg Squat Balance** (Hold each position ten counts)
- **Balance Shift** (Hold each position Six to Ten counts)
- **Quarter Eagle** x 3 Right & 3 Left with 10 yard sprint & return
- **Z Band** x 2 each drill a) Plant & Cut b) Plant & Cut & Return c) Stepover (Inside foot)
- **Hoops Double** In 6 x 6 hoops
- **Flag Series** x 2 of each drill
- **Speed/Agility Ladder Routine** (Choose six drills, 3 repetitions of each)
- **Little Hurdles** – Even 6 x 6 hurdles
- **One Eighty Jumps** x 3 Right & 3 Left

SATURDAY
- **Warm-up #2**
- **Two Player Weave** x 2 @ 20 yards
- **Follow the leader** x 2 @ 20 yards
- **Ball Drop** – Two Balls x 4
- **Reaction Run** x 4 @ 10 yards
- **Scrimmage** 11v. 11

Training Phase: In-season   **Objective: Raise intensity & lower volume of work**

MONDAY (SAS Emphasis)
- **Warm-up #1**
- **Stagger Start** x 3 Right & 3 Left @ 20 yards
- **Balance Start** x 3 Right & 3 Left @ 20 yards
- **Running Start** 3 Right & 3 Left @ 15 yards
- **Dancing Start** 2 Right & 2 Left @ 20 yards
- **Jump & Go** 2 Right & 2 Left @ 20 yards
- **Ninety Degree Jumps** x 3 Right & 3 Left – Head the ball on each rep

TUESDAY (LSA Emphasis)
- **Warm-up #2**
- **Single Leg Squat Balance** (Hold each position ten counts)
- **Balance Shift** (Hold each position six to ten counts)
- **Hoops Double** In 6 x 6 hoops
- **Speed/Agility Ladder Routine** (Choose six drills, 3 repetitions of each)
- **Little Hurdles** - Even 4 x 6 hurdles

WEDNESDAY
- **Warm-up #2**
- **Numbered Cones** x 6
- **Three Player Weave** x 3 @ 30 yards
- **Reaction Run** x 6 @ 10 yards
- **Ball drop** – Two Balls x 6

THURSDAY (SAS Emphasis)
- **Warm-up #1**
- **Running Start** 3 Right & 3 Left @ 15 yards
- **Dancing Start** 2 Right & 2 Left @ 20 yards
- **Jump & Go** 2 Right & 2 Left @ 20 yards
- **One Eighty Jumps** x 3 Right & 3 Left – Head the ball on each rep

FRIDAY (LSA emphasis)
- **Warm-up #2**
- **Single Leg Squat Balance** (Hold each position ten counts)
- **Balance Shift** (Hold each position six to ten counts)
- **Hoops Double** In 4 x 6 hoops
- **Speed/Agility Ladder Routine** (Choose four drills, 2 repetitions of each)

SATURDAY
Game

Training Phase: Off-season   Objective: High volume

MONDAY (SAS Emphasis)
- **Warm-up** #1
- **Soccer Start** x 3 @ 15 yards
- **Stagger Stance** x 3 Right & 3 Left @ 20 yards
- **Balance Start** x 3 Right & 3 Left @ 20 yards
- **Running Start** 3 Right & 3 Left @ 15 yards
- **Sidestep & Go** 2 Right & 2 Left @ 20 yards
- **Crossover Step & Go** 2 Right & 2 Left @ 20 yards
- **Scramble Out** (Start prone Position) x 3 @ 20 yards
- **Seat Roll & Go** 2 Right and 2 Left @ 10 yards
- **Plant & Drive Off** Left x 3 Right & 3 Left @ 15 yards
- **Jump & Go** @ 10 yards x 3
- **180 Jump & Go** 2 Right and 2 Left @ 10 yards
- **Sled or Tire Pull** x 6 @ 20 yards

TUESDAY (LSA Emphasis)
- **Warm-up** #2
- **Single Leg Squat Balance** (Hold each position ten counts)
- **Balance Shift** (Hold each position six to ten counts)
- **Z Band** x 3 of each drill a) Plant & Cut b) Plant & Cut & Return c) Stepover (Inside foot)
- **Flag** Series x 3 of each drill
- **Speed/Agility Ladder Routine** (Chose four drills, 3 repetitions of each)
- **Little Hurdles** 6 x 6 hurdles
- **Cobra Drills** (Two Bands) 8 x 30 seconds – 1 minute recovery

WEDNESDAY
- **Warm-up** #2
- **Decision Making Start** x 4 @ 10 yards
- **Three Player Weave** x 4 @ 30 yards
- **Speed/Agility Ladder Routine** (Chose six drills, 3 repetitions of each)
- **Parachute** 6 x 40 yards forward, 3 x 20 yards backward

THURSDAY (SAS Emphasis)
- **Warm-up** #1
- **Soccer Start** x 3 @ 15 yards
- **Stagger Stance** x 4 Right & 4 Left @ 10 yards
- **Balance Start** x 4 Right & 4 Left @ 10 yards
- **Running Start** x 4 Right & 4 Left @ 10 yards
- **Plant & Drive Off** left x 3 Right & 3 Left @ 10 yards
- **Push & Go** x 3@ 10 yards
- **Shoulder Bump & Go** 3 @ 15 yards
- **Jump & Go** @ 10 yards x 3
- **180 Jump & Go** 2 Right and 2 Left @ 10 yards
- **Two Hops & Sprint** at 15 yards x 2 off Right & Left foot
- **Four Bounds into Sprint** @ 20 yards x 2 off Right & Left foot
- **Sled or Tire Pull** x 6 @ 20 yards

FRIDAY (LSA emphasis)
- **Warm-up** #2
- **Single Leg Squat Balance** (Hold each position ten counts)
- **Balance Shift** (Hold each position six to ten counts)
- **Z Band** x 2 of each drill a) Plant & Cut b) Plant & Cut & Return c) Stepover (Inside foot)
- **Flag Series** x 2 of each drill
- **Speed/Agility Ladder Routine** (Choose eight drills, 2 repetitions of each)
- **Little Hurdles** – Broken 6 x 8 hurdles
- **Cobra drills** (Two bands) 10 x 15 seconds – 30 seconds recovery

SATURDAY
- **Warm-up** #2
- **Decision Making Start** x 6
- **Three Player Weave** x 4 @ 30 yards
- **Speed/Agility Ladder Routine** (Choose six drills, 2 repetitions of each)
- **Parachute** x 8 @ 60 yards forward – 4 x 30 yards backward

Training Phase: Pre-season   Objective: Raise intensity of work, maintain volume

MONDAY (SAS Emphasis)
- **Warm-up** #1
- **Stagger Stance** x 2 Right & 2 Left @ 20 yards
- **Balance Start** x 2 Right & 2 Left @ 20 yards
- **Running Start** 4 Right & 4 Left @ 15 yards
- **Sidestep & Go** 3 Right & 3 Left @ 20 yards
- **Crossover step** & Go 2 Right & 2 Left @ 20 yards
- **Scramble Out** (Start prone Position) x 3 @ 20 yards
- **Seat Roll & Go** 2 right and 2 left @ 10 yards
- **Plant & Drive Off** x 3 Right & 3 Left @ 15 yards
- **Push & Go** x 3@ 15 yards
- **Shoulder Bump & Go** 3 @ 15 yards
- **Jump & Go** @ 10 yards x 3
- **180 Jump & Go** 2 Right and 2 Left @ 10 yards
- **Two Hops & Sprint** at 15 yards x 2 Off Right & Left foot
- **Four Bounds into Sprint** @ 20 yards x 2 Off Right & Left foot

TUESDAY (LSA Emphasis)
- **Warm-up** #2
- **Single Leg Squat Balance** (Hold each position ten counts)
- **Balance Shift** (Hold each position six to ten counts)
- **Z Band** 2 x each drill a) Plant & Cut b) Plant & Cut & Return c) Stepover (Inside foot)
- **Flag Series** 2 x each drill
- **Speed/Agility Ladder Routine** (Choose five drills, 3 repetitions of each)
- **Cobra Drills** (Two bands) 6 x 30 sec- 1 minute recovery

WEDNESDAY
- **Warm-up** #2
- **Ball Drop** – Two Ball x 6 – Play the ball on one bounce
- **Reaction Runs** x 6 @ 10 yards
- **Three Player Weave** x 4 @ 30 yards
- **Speed/Agility Ladder Routine** (Choose five drills, 3 repetitions of each)
- **Parachute** 6 x60 yards forward – 3 x30 yards backward

THURSDAY (SAS Emphasis)
- **Warm-up** #1
- **Stagger Stance** x 2 Right & 2 Left @ 20 yards
- **Balance Start** x 2 Right & 2 Left @ 20 yards
- **Running Start** 3 Right & 3 Left @ 15 yards
- **Plant & Drive Off** left x 3 Right & 3 Left @ 15 yards
- **Push & Go** x 3@ 15 yards
- **Shoulder Bump & Go** 3 @ 15 yards
- **Jump & Go** @ 10 yards x 3
- **180 Jump & Go** 2 Right and 2 Left @ 10 yards
- **Two Hops & Sprint** at 15 yards x 2 off Right & Left foot
- **Four Bounds into Sprint** @ 20 yards x 2 Off Right & Left foot

FRIDAY (LSA emphasis)
- **Warm-up** #2
- **Single Leg Squat Balance** (Hold each position ten counts)
- **Balance Shift** (Hold each position six to ten counts
- **Speed/Agility Ladder Routine** (Choose five drills, 2 repetitions of each)
- **Cobra Drills** (One Band) 8-10 seconds – 30 seconds recovery

SATURDAY
Scrimmage

ELITE

MONDAY (SAS Emphasis)
- **Warm-up #1**
- **Running Start** 3 Right & 3 Left @ 15 yards
- **Sidestep & Go** 2 Right & 2 Left @ 20 yards
- **Crossover Step & Go** 2 Right & 2 Left @ 20 yards
- **Jump & Go** @ 10 yards x 3
- **180 Jump & Go** 2 Right and 2 Left @ 10 yards
- **Two Hops & Sprint** at 15 yards x 2 off Right & Left foot
- **Four Bounds into Sprint** @ 20 yards x 2 off Right & Left foot

TUESDAY (LSA Emphasis)
- **Warm-up #2**
- **Single Leg Squat Balance** (Hold each position ten counts)
- **Balance Shift** (Hold each position six to ten counts)
- **Z Band** 2 of each drill a) Plant & Cut b) Plant & Cut & Return c) Stepover (Inside foot)
- **Flag Series** 2 of each drill

WEDNESDAY
- **Warm-up #2**
- **Ball Drop** – Two Ball x 6
- **Reaction Runs** x 6 @ 10 yards
- **Three Player Weave** x 3 @ 30 yards
- **Speed/Agility Ladder Routine** (Choose Six drills, 3 repetitions of each)

THURSDAY (SAS Emphasis)
- **Warm-up #1**
- **Running Start** 3 Right & 3 Left @ 15 yards
- **Plant & Drive Off** left x 3 Right & 3 Left @ 15 yards
- **Push & Go** x 3@ 15 yards
- **Shoulder Bump & Go** 3 @ 15 yards
- **Jump & Go** @ 10 yds x 3
- **180 Jump & Go** 2 Right and 2 Left @ 10 yards

FRIDAY (LSA emphasis)
- **Warm-up #2**
- **Single Leg Squat Balance** (Hold each position ten counts)
- **Balance Shift** (Hold each position six to ten counts)
- **Speed/Agility Ladder Routine** (Choose four drills, 3 repetitions of each)

SATURDAY
Game

TESTING AND EVALUATION

Testing and evaluation should be viewed as an essential feedback mechanism in speed training. Testing should be used to establish a baseline, to measure progress from training period to training period as well as from year to year.

In order to achieve positive feedback and learn from the test(s) it is necessary to have a specific purpose for the tests. It is best to use tests to determine an athlete's strengths and weaknesses relative to the demands of that particular player's position. Once this is established, testing can direct the training to the essential activities in order to optimize training. Testing can be used to see how the player compares to other players as well to see how the player compares to past players at similar stages in their career. This is a tremendous aid in goal setting and a positive motivation for the player.

Tests must be valid and reliable. To be valid, the test must measure what it is intended to test. Reliability refers to the ability of a test to consistently measure a given factor. In order to do this the tests must be administered in exactly the same way each time. For speed and lateral speed and agility tests it is preferable to have them electronically timed. This ensures accuracy. If at all possible, it is helpful to have the same person administer the same test each time.

Tests must be easily administered and interpreted. The instructions and the expected outcome should be simple and clear to both the test administrator and the athlete. If the test is not easily interpreted, the athlete will not relate to it and not give a good effort on the test. In addition the tests should require a minimum of equipment.

TIMING PROCEDURES

Electronic
Sensor placed at mid foreleg height for the start. Sensor placed at waist height for the finish.

Hand
Start watch when the first foot touches down over the starting line. Stop the watch when the torso breaks the plane of the finish - do not anticipate the finish.

Round the time up to the next tenth of a second and indicate that it is a hand time by placing a small h after the time. For example a 4.71 will round up to a 4.8h.

THE TESTS

SPEED TESTS

10 Meter or 10 Yard Standing Start

Test starting off both the right and the left foot in order to see if there is a significant difference between the two feet. Starting position should be a stride stance with the front foot closest to the starting line. Run through the finish line ten yards from the start.

10 Meter or 10 Yard Flying Start

Use a 20 meter or 20 yard run in to the ten yard testing distance. To test top end speed.

40 Meter or 40 Yard Sprint

Use a standing start off of the players preferred starting foot.

AGILITY TESTS

Ajax 50 Yard Shuttle

— *see illustration*

Start off of the preferred starting foot. The player must touch one foot on the line each time. Run and touch line at ten yards, plant foot and turn and run back toward the start line. Repeat five times for a total of fifty yards.

Agility 5-10-5

— *see illustration*

To test change of direction ability. To determine the ability to move both right and left. Start to the left of the center line, sprint to the right and touch a foot on the line at 5 yards (A). Sprint back to the left to a line at 10 yards and touch a foot on the line (B) and sprint back through the start line (C). Repeat the same test to the left. The agility score is the sum of the best scores right and left.

Myrland Star Test

— *see illustration*

A test to determine the athlete's ability to move to the right and compare movement to the left based on the wheel principle. Start with the left hand on cone one for testing in a clockwise direction. Use a self start and run to touch center cone. Start the watch when the player takes their hand off cone one. After touching center cone run out to touch cone two and return to the center. Repeat the process until the player touches cone one. Stop the watch when the player touches cone one.

ANAEROBIC POWER & CAPACITY TESTS

300 Yard Shuttle

Twenty five yards in length. Six times

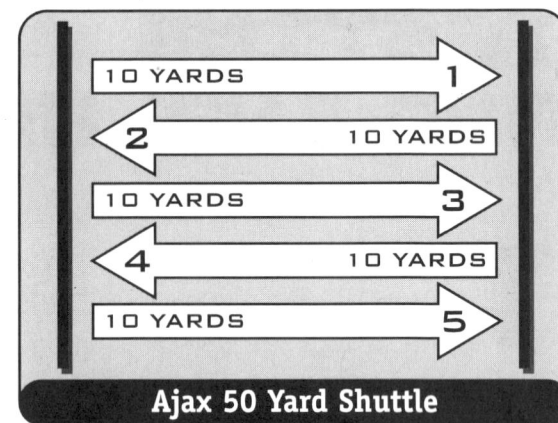

Ajax 50 Yard Shuttle

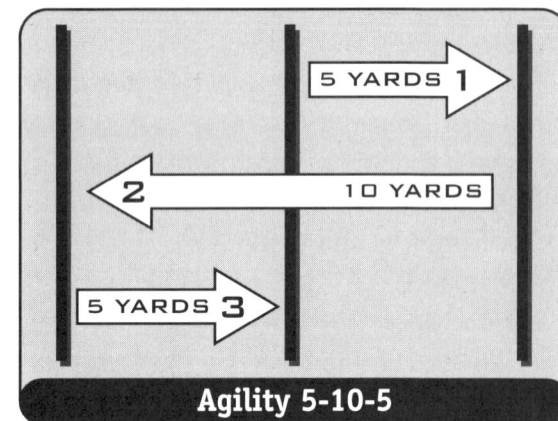

Agility 5-10-5

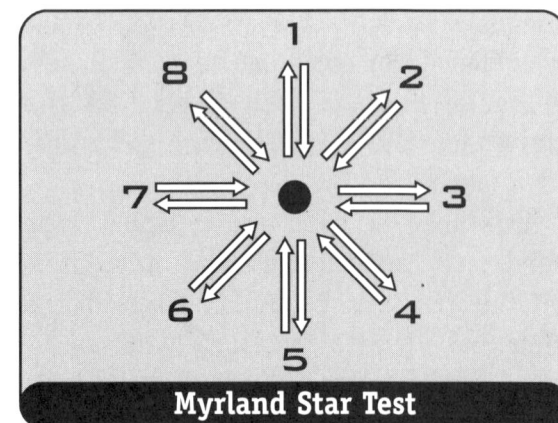

Myrland Star Test

down and back. Three minutes recovery before a second run. The score is the average time of the two runs. Also note the difference in time between the two runs: this is a good fatigue index.

POWER TESTS

Squat Jump
The athlete starts in a squat position. No movement is allowed. The athletes jumps up and reaches as high as possible. The height of the jump is determined by the difference between the reach and the height jumped.

Counter Movement Vertical Jump
Also known as the Sergeant Jump. The athlete crouches down and then jumps up as high as possible. The height of the jump is determined by the difference between the reach and the height jumped.

15 Second Repetitive Jump Test
Count the number of maximal jumps that the player can achieve in fifteen seconds.

Standing Long Jump
With a two foot takeoff, jump out as far as possible. Start in a standing position with the toes behind the scratch line. Crouch down and jump out as far as possible. Measure from the takeoff line to the

heel(s) nearest the takeoff.

Five Hops Right and Left
Compare the distance from left to right. More than one foot distance between the two is unacceptable.

30 Sec Cone Jump
The athlete jumps side to side over 12 inch cone as many times as possible in thirty seconds. Player stands on the right side (facing counter) of four 12 inch cones lined up in a row. On the command "GO" the athlete will double leg jump side to side over the cones for 30 seconds. Count every foot contact. Jumps in progress do not count. The starting commands are "READY – GO." Tell the athlete when 15 seconds have elapsed and every 5 seconds until 30 seconds. Ending command is "READY - STOP."

Overback Medicine Ball
Triple Extension Throw
The athlete swings the ball down between their legs and throws the ball over the back projecting the implement as far as possible by extending the legs and the trunk. Use a three kilo medicine ball. Start in a standing position with the toes behind the scratch line. Crouch down and jump out as far as possible. Measure from the foul line to the point of first contact of the ball. Use a three kilo medicine ball.

Forward Through the Legs
Medicine Ball Throw
The athlete swings the ball down between their legs and throws the ball forward through the legs projecting the implement by extending the legs and the trunk. Measure from the foul line to the point of first contact of the ball. Use a three kilo medicine ball.

APPENDIX A - EQUIPMENT LIST

Trainer
Harness- Bullet belt
Sled
Overspeed trainer
Parachute
Reaction Coach™
Speed/Agility Ladder
Acceleration Ladder
Hoops
Mini Bands
Mini Hurdles – 6" & 12"
Cones
Numbered Cones
Medicine Balls
Electronic Timer – Speed Trap
Reaction Belt
Z Ball
Jump Rope
Low Box 4"
Flags
Weight Vest

APPENDIX B - ADDITIONAL RESOURCES

BOOKS AND ARTICLES

Bangsbo, Jens. **Fitness Training In Football – A Scientific Approach**. Bagsvaerd, Denmark: HO+ Storm. 1994.

Dick, Frank. **Sprints and Relays**. London: British Amateur Athletic Board. 1987.

Dominguez, Richard H. M.D., and Gajda, Robert S. **Total Body Training**. New York, NY: Warner Books. 1982.

Drabik, Jo'zef Ph.D. **Children & Sports Training**. Island Pond, Vermont: Stadion Publishing Company, Inc. 1996.

Harre, Dietrich, Dr., Editor. **Principles of Sports Training: Introduction to The Theory and Methods of Training**. Berlin: Sportverlag. 1982.

Kurz, Thomas., **Science of Sports Training**, Island Pont, Vt: Stadion Publishing Company, 1991

Kurz, Thomas. **Stretching Scientifically – A Guide to Flexibility Training**. Third Edition. Island Pont, Vt: Stadion Publishing Company. 1994.

Kreighbaum, Ellen and Barthels, Katharine M. **Biomechanics - A Qualitative Approach For Studying Human Movement**. Fourth Edition. Boston, Allyn and Bacon. 1996.

Mac Dougall, J. Duncan., Wenger, Howard A., Green, Howard J., Editors. **Physiological Testing of the Elite Athlete**. Second Edition. Champaign, Illinois: Human Kinetics Books, Inc. 1991.

McFarlane, Brent. **The Science of Hurdling**, Canadian Track and Field Association. 1988.

Pyke, Frank S. **Better Coaching – Advanced Coaching Manual**. Belconnen, Australia: Australian Coaching Council. 1991.

Reilly, T. Secher, N. Snell, P. and Williams, C. **Physiology of Sports**. London: E & FN Spon. 1990.

Rushall, Brent S., and Pyke, Frank S. **Training for Sports and Fitness**. South Melbourne: Macmillan Education Australia PTY LTD. 1990.

Verheijen, Raymond. **Conditioning For Soccer**. Spring City, Pennsylvania: Reedswain Videos and Books. 1998.

Seeveren, Tjeu and Kormelink, Henry. **The Coaching Philosophies of Louis Van Gall and The Ajax Coaches**. Leeuwarden, The Netherlands: Uitgeverij Eisma.

VIDEOS

Gambetta, Vern and Odgers, Steve. **The Complete Guide to Medicine Ball Training Video.**

Gambetta, Vern and Odgers, Steve. **Jump, Jump, Jump Plyometrics Video.**

Gambetta, Vern and Odgers, Steve. **Training for Sport-Specific Speed Video: Straight Ahead Speed.**

Gambetta, Vern and Odgers, Steve. **Training for Sport-Specific Speed Video: Lateral Speed and Agility.**

Gambetta, Vern and Myrland, Steve. **Speed/Agility Ladder Footwork Drills.**

Gambetta, Vern. **The 3S System™: Soccer Speed Video.**

Gambetta, Vern & Wegerle, Roy. **Soccer Fit - Functional Conditioning for Soccer - Speed, Agility, Strength & Stamina.**

Gambetta, Vern and Odgers, Steve. **Circuit Training.**

Gambetta, Vern. **Proprioceptive Plyometrics.**